MADE IN BRAZIL

ONE WOMAN'S STORY OF BEING MOULDED INTO
THE BEAUTY OF GOD'S IMAGE THROUGH HER CALLING

By
Shirley Hough

Disclaimer

Please note that in preparing this work, I have attempted to describe events and locations and, in many instances, had to create conversations from my memories of what happened at the time. To protect their identity, I have changed the names of many individuals and places.

All Scripture quotations are taken from the NKJV.

Scripture quotations are from the *New King James Version*. Copyright © 1982 by Thomas Nelson Inc. Used by permission. All rights reserved.

Shirley Hough asserts her moral right to be identified as the author of this book.

All rights reserved. No part of this publication may be reproduced, distributed, or transmitted in any form or by any means, including photocopying, recording or other electronic or mechanical methods, without the prior written permission of the publisher, except in the case of brief quotations in critical reviews and certain other non-commercial uses permitted by copyright law.

First published May 2024

© 2024 by Shirley Hough

British Library Cataloguing in Publication Data

A CIP catalogue record for this book is available from the British Library.

ISBN: 9-78173-9614881

Editorial and publishing services by The Heritage Publishers Ltd
Cover Design by Ije Designs

THANK YOU

I want to thank all those who nudged and encouraged me to write my story, spurred me on and contributed to making this a reality.

Thanks to each one who saw my potential, believed in me and inspired me.

To my financial and prayer supporters down through the years, this is your story, too. I think of David's battle with the Amalekites in 1 Samuel 30:24, *"...But as his part is who goes down to battle, so shall his part be who stays by the supplies; they shall share alike."* Those holding the fort were as much a part of the team as those who went to the battle frontlines. Without you behind the scenes, I would never be where I am today. The kids' lives and mine have been impacted and changed because of you, and I am eternally grateful.

To the faithful crowd of witnesses walking alongside me, especially those who picked me up, ministered to me and got me back on my feet in the toughest moments when I was wounded in battle, thank you.

Thank you to the team at UFM Worldwide for taking me on to work in Brazil and caring for and facilitating life for us, your mission partners, in many ways.

Above all, I thank my Heavenly Father for taking care of me and all the details along this journey. To him be all the glory, honour, and praise forever.

TABLE OF CONTENTS

Thank you iii

Introduction: My Story, His Story 1

Chapter One: Clay in the Hands of the Potter 5

Chapter Two: A Divine Appointment 9

Chapter Three: Refiners Fire 16

Chapter Four: Ready For Anything 30

Chapter Five: Stepping into the Unknown 41

Chapter Six: Holding Fast to the Call 51

Chapter Seven: Adventures and Challenges 62

Chapter Eight: Lives we have Touched 72

Chapter Nine: God sets the Solitary in Families 87

Chapter Ten: Rescuing Hope 96

Chapter Eleven: "Gringa" in the Interior 103

Chapter Twelve: The Valley of the Shadow of Death...... 114

Chapter Thirteen: Their Stories Told 120

Chapter Fourteen: Living by Faith 133

Chapter Fifteen: Grace goes Deeper Still 140

Chapter Sixteen: Tested By Fire 150

Chapter Seventeen: Covenant Love 168

Chapter Eighteen: Serve You While I Am Waiting 174

Conclusion 195

Recommended Reading 199

INTRODUCTION

MY STORY, HIS STORY

"She's a publisher."

The unexpected words went straight to my heart. I was completely unprepared. I had just been introduced to someone at a prayer meeting and was not thinking about my book.

Suddenly, my thoughts were taken elsewhere, a commotion of feelings whirling through my mind. *Was this the moment? Was I ready for this? I hadn't had time to think about it.*

Over ten years ago, God challenged me to write my story as a testimony to all that he had done on my thirty-five-year life journey at that point. It had been a journey of positive and negative experiences, highs and lows, joys and sadness, trials and difficulties, victories and blessings.

I wrote it and then, due to circumstances, allowed it to sit dormant. Close friends nudged me along the way, but I had lost my confidence.

Then, out of the blue, God put a publisher right before me!

Surely, this was not a coincidence but a divine appointment. I had come to recognize these many times on my journey. It was now or never! I had to take the plunge.

With no time to think about it, when the meeting finished, I told her about my book.

"We have to get your story out there; these stories need to be told!" was her response.

I knew she was right.

Walking home, I had some things to think about. Life had just taken a real turn!

The truth was, my story had remained dormant because I didn't want any further exposure.

The next day, on a long walk along the river where I go to think and pray, I laid it before the Lord, remembering my own words to my daughters and others;

> "God is the author of our lives. He is writing our stories, ordaining our circumstances, and weaving our paths."

Introduction: My Story, His Story

As I walked, his voice came clearly to my heart -

> *"This is MY story! Don't be timid to expose it. I have written it the way it is because this is the story that I want to be told. Others need to know, and it needs to be published and put out there. It is a ministry you must release and make known so I can touch and minister to others."*

I was convicted and uncomfortable. God takes us out of our comfort zones to make us trust him and step out in faith wherever he leads, without limitations.

It was no mistake that he had brought this publisher into my life. The book was no longer to remain dormant. The story had to be told. I surrendered everything afresh.

> *'Lord, give me the courage to do it,' I prayed. 'I want to hold nothing back. May my story be told to your glory, fulfilling all your plans and purposes in doing so.'*

Life is an untapped reservoir of vast experiences, which God uses if we yield to him. Whatever happens on the journey is needed. Nothing is lost or wasted with God. Each situation is to bring us to where we are now.

So, in giving you my (God's) story, I release the wealth he deposited in my life to be used rather than wasted. I pray that

God will touch, challenge, minister to, inspire and encourage you to respond to his purpose.

My desire is that you become fully aware of how much God is interested in YOU - who you are and who you will become. Your personal story is also being written, and things are allowed to happen by his sovereign will and higher purpose.

May he stir up in you a desire to know him and be ALL that he intended.

ALL that I am, have, and ever hope to be is for you, Jesus.

CHAPTER ONE

CLAY IN THE HANDS OF THE POTTER

4th September 1976, 03.00am

A young mother gazed at her healthy 6lbs 12oz baby girl, little imagining what lay ahead. That baby Shirley would one day leave the comforts of home in cold, grey Britain for the hot, sticky tropics of Northern Brazil.

The path would not be easy or straight forward, but it was God-ordained. God knew and formed Shirley in her mother's womb according to his perfect design and purposes. Knowing her every moment before anyone else, he marked and ordained his blueprint for her life.

Like clay in the potter's hands, Shirley would be moulded, broken, and made into a vessel that would practice two key words in reaching her fullest potential – Trust and Obedience. In blind faith, holding on to God's Word without considering the consequence or outcome, she learned that his way is perfect but not always clear-cut or logical.

Through times of brokenness and deep pain, this vessel would also learn that this was God's will and purpose, and as she was broken, his beautiful treasure would be poured out on those around her.

God called her to the mission field, not to *serve* and to *do* for him but to refine and make her a beautiful vessel and treasure to reflect him, be poured out and transformed into his glory.

> *"But we have this treasure in earthen vessels that the excellence of the power may be of God and not of us."*
> 2 Corinthians 4:7

God longs to know and refine you, too. The refining process can be painful and unpleasant. However, it will draw you closer to him, so let him make, break and mould YOU into his image, according to his blueprint, so that his beauty and treasure within you can overflow and radiate within your small corner of the world.

So, just how was this foundation and blueprint laid?

I was the firstborn of five to Christian parents who influenced us with God's Word, Christian principles and church activity from our early years. We were a close-knit family, with hours of fun, laughter and plenty of adventure, characterized by much activity, including picnics, walks, holidays in the countryside, on the family farm, or seaside resorts. Mum stayed home and was always there for us, while Dad, the hard-working engineer, always sought the best for his young family, with strict discipline and plenty of rules.

The demands of family life were more difficult during my teenage years. As the eldest and guinea pig in many new experiences, I was more independent as my mum cared for the younger ones, resulting in internal conflict and struggles, timidity and low self-esteem. Looking back, I realize these preparatory years made me strong and forced me to grow, persevere, and become self-reliant, with the strengthened character needed for the tough days and toil on the mission field.

I made a childlike commitment to Christ at a Billy Graham crusade when I was 8 years old, followed by a good life of church activity, but it was at a Harvest ministry youth camp that my spiritual journey started, and an encounter with God would turn my life around.

On my 17th birthday, as the preacher spoke about the Cross, the reality of what Christ had done dawned on me as I heard about the cruel sufferings he endured because he loved and wanted to offer forgiveness to me. Everything I had heard over the years suddenly became real. Several issues and problems in my life were predominantly linked to unforgiveness and rebellion, but the depth of Christ's sacrifice in giving up his life would bring freedom and forgiveness. That night, I saw my sin as the barrier to an authentic Christian life, and I had done nothing in return for all God had done for me.

> "If Jesus Christ be Lord and died for me, then NO sacrifice is too great for me to make for him[1]."
> – C.T. Studd

Broken before God through conviction, I repented of my sin, sought forgiveness and surrendered my life to him as a living sacrifice[1].

It was a birthday that would not be forgotten!

It was time for a complete turnaround. The decision changed my life and brought direction, conviction, deep joy, and peace like I had never known.

This decision started an adventure I never dreamt I could embark on, and I certainly never imagined where it would lead!

---

[1] Romans 12:1

CHAPTER TWO

A DIVINE APPOINTMENT

It was another Tuesday night. I was at the bus stop in the dark and cold, waiting for the blue Peugeot, my lift to the children's club in West Benwell, Newcastle.

This was my weekly Tuesday routine since meeting the Faith Mission Area workers from Ireland, who had started attending our church in County Durham. Mum, being an Irish woman, made the link and connected our two families. Yet this connection was no mistake but a divine appointment that would bring about another turning point in God's story.

At the time, I was training to be a nursery nurse while teaching in Sunday school.

Then, in the summer of 1995, Andrew invited me to help at my first Faith Mission camp in Morecambe. From there, I got involved in the children and young people's work in a difficult area of Newcastle.

It was my preparation and training ground for many situations I would later encounter. These were kids from broken homes who really had to count the cost to follow Jesus in their difficult backgrounds and circumstances.

One night, he taught from the passage about turning the other cheek when somebody wrongs us[2].

But this will cost these girls and be practically impossible. I thought. *If they turned the other cheek at school or it was known that they went to church, they would be mocked and beaten up.*

In fact, they had to fight back in self-defence to survive. Such was the brutality of their life at school.

"We had an affectionate name for Shirley; "Mighty Mouse."

Why?

She was as quiet as a church mouse, but God used her mightily.

Shirley was just like a magnet – a channel for the Lord. As soon as the kids entered, they gravitated towards her, and she always had time to sit and chat. Without being upfront, she ministered to them quietly but powerfully. This was the same at the club or at camp."

- Andrew

---

[2] Matthew 5:39

A Divine Appointment

I loved and greatly looked forward to those precious opportunities to practice what I was learning at college for my diploma in Nursery Nursing - caring for young children, understanding their developmental needs, and preparing appropriate educational opportunities. The only difference is that I was learning now how to teach children within a Bible club context.

I met people there who knew what it was to intercede, saw my potential and, thank God, encouraged me. These people have greatly impacted and influenced my life till today. The leader at the time is now in her nineties. We still meet regularly to have fellowship, pray and chat. She spurred me on, and her faithfulness to God's work, despite limitations with her sight, hearing, and walking, has greatly impacted me.

Andrew's life radiated Christ. He was a warm, caring, down-to-earth man who brought God to life as he taught the children and left an impact wherever he went. God used him to teach me and stir up a desire for what he had. Shouldn't we leave a legacy and imprint on others? This was the example I wanted to follow!

My daily life was varied with practical experiences through my course, nannying, assisting in nurseries and schools, helping children with special needs, church-related youth activities, and Girls Brigade leadership training. My horizons broadened as I became more independent.

Did God have something else in mind?

It was difficult to find a job after my nursery nurse college training, and the conviction grew in my heart that God had something different planned. I eventually worked as a nanny, looking after two young girls. However, I kept feeling God wanted me to go beyond helping at Faith Mission clubs and camps. He wanted me to attend Bible College and train to become fully involved in missions. The thought terrified me for several reasons—I didn't want to leave my home comforts in Durham, the familiar, friends, family, and the activities I enjoyed.

Upheaval? No thanks!

Secondly, Bible College seemed boring and old-fashioned. I could never envisage myself there. The more the thoughts came to mind, the more I pushed away and avoided facing them.

When God is in something, he doesn't let us escape. Remember Jonah? He kept running from God's instructions. But God pursues us until we are willing to listen and obey. This was my case as a leader at the Faith Mission

A Divine Appointment

summer camps in July 1996, nearer home in Esh Winning. God gripped my attention, and I couldn't escape....

Characteristically, I sleep well and deeply, and lying awake at night is rare. However, the lessons taught, memory verses, and the songs we sang kept challenging me.

I couldn't avoid the call

God had a plan for me, something only I could do. I needed to surrender to these plans and live for him.

One night, I simply could not sleep. I kept waking up with verses on my mind.

"Go into all the world and preach the gospel[3]*...*

and lo, I am with YOU always[4]*."*

"Go, am I not sending YOU? Go in the strength of the Lord[5]*."*

The words came to me strongly, and I felt like Samuel when God kept calling him until he responded, "Speak, for your servant hears."[6].

God's voice was clear, but my will was not yielded. The kids were sleeping, and I was so restless that I got up, went

---

[3] Mark 16:15
[4] Matthew 28:19-20
[5] Judges 6:14
[6] 1 Samuel 3:10

into the toilets and wrestled with giving in to what God was asking of me. It was my first encounter with the struggle when God would speak contrary to my wants and desires. But the experience became very familiar over the years.

I had to obey God and trust that he knew best for my life. So that night, I finally gave in and, to seal my decision, shared what had happened with the leaders the following day.

****

With my application to Faith Mission Bible College, another landmark of my spiritual journey was in place. I took the decision in obedience, but, oh, the emotional mixture that followed: fear, worries, feelings of inadequacy and much more.

Obedience, yes, but at great cost. Could I, timid as I was, give up everything I'd ever known? But I had to learn to lean on God like never before. The way ahead was unknown, new, and unfamiliar. I was to leave my job and live by faith, trusting him to provide my every need and living out the reality of his promises. He alone would help me to cope every step of the way.

My God NEVER fails, as I learned each day.

A Divine Appointment

The Faith Mission had Prayer Unions, groups that prayed for their work. Andrew invited me to one group that usually met in Langley Moor, which also impacted my life greatly. At my Prayer Union farewell in Sept 1997, Andrew quoted the verse God had used to call me at camp, Matthew 28:19-20:

"Go therefore and make disciples of all the nations.... and lo I am with you always" (in Hebrew, it reads as "I with you AM"). How much more secure could I be? I was within the great I AM. He was with me. What more did I need? Why would I fear? I wasn't alone; I was going with the Lord God Almighty.

My leaving service at church, organised by the Faith Mission, took place in September 1997 before I headed to college in Edinburgh. I'll never forget that night's message.

'Then He said to them, "Follow Me, and I will make you fishers of men."' – Matthew 4:19. The preacher took his text in a form I'd never perceived before. "I will make YOU." As the years went on, I finally understood that message. God wasn't just asking me to reach others. He was calling me to make ME, Shirley, into a new vessel.

Faith Mission Bible College was where God began to refine me, and the foundations were laid for much more ahead.

CHAPTER THREE

REFINERS FIRE

I was so scared. Everything within me wanted to turn and run!

On the day we pulled up outside the college, I was filled with nerves, stepping into what would be my new home for the next two years. There on the college steps were two Irish girls from Cork, Hazel and Fiona.

I discovered I was to share a room with Hazel. Both girls became lifelong friends, with whom I laughed and cried throughout college, as links in the chain of my being made into who God wanted me to be and lifetime foundations were laid.

∞∞∞∞∞∞∞∞

"That first term, Shirley and Hazel shared a room. We spent a lot of time together and bonded on several levels. We were at the Bible College to learn more about God and His

Word, grow in our relationship with Him and learn to pray and minister effectively. With these spiritual desires in common, we shared our hearts, listened to one another's stories and struggles, and prayed with each other, creating a deep and trusting bond that endures today.

We also bonded because we had fun together and enjoyed each other's company. We loved to have the craic[7] and a good laugh, usually at one another's expense! We soon discovered a humorous character with a genius for practical jokes under Shirley's seemingly quiet

"It was September 1997, and I was beginning my second year at the Faith Mission Bible College in Edinburgh. H and I had been out, and on walking up the steps to the front door, we introduced ourselves to a new first year student, on the way out with her parents. FMBC was known for more conservative dressing, but we were casually dressed. Shirley was relieved to see two "normal" looking girls, and we had a good laugh about it. Over the weeks and months, we became firm friends, and twenty-five years later, we are close sisters who have supported each other through hard times, despite the geographical distance between us."
- Fiona

---

[7] enjoyable social activity

exterior. (Shirley, I can't remember who did what to whom, but there was shaving foam, leaping out of cupboards in the dark, a broken bed leg upheld by a paint can, and exiting to the chip shop through windows....) It was not all serious highbrow studies at the college; there were plenty of shenanigans!

Being from the south of Ireland, Hazel and I didn't go back home during mid-term breaks, and Shirley often invited us to Durham, where her family welcomed us and looked after us. It meant so much when I was so far away from my own family.

Those years cemented our friendship. We may not be in touch often or see each other for years, but once we are together, it is like no time has passed. We can count on each other to pray and offer advice and support. The friendship is fresh, and the fellowship is sweet. According to Proverbs 17:17, *"A friend loves at all times"*. I am grateful to have a friend like that." - Fiona

College days were very full.

Monday to Thursday began with morning devotions, with different students assigned to lead each day. We memorised one Bible verse a day, and the staff then picked a student to recite it during devotions. We had to be ready as we never knew who would be chosen! Then, we recited them in groups of up to 50 to someone designated to test us. What a challenge! This practice and reading through the Bible every year were prerequisites for completing and graduating from the course. Subsequently, we had lectures until lunchtime, studying subjects such as Church History, a Panoramic View of the Old Testament, books of the Bible, Greek, Doctrine, and Apologetics.

Friday mornings were set aside for staff and students to seek God and intercede for specific needs. On Monday afternoons, we were assigned practical jobs to help with the college's general maintenance and upkeep. The other afternoons and evenings were dedicated to study and weekly assignments.

After tea, we prayed around the tables for different regions, the Faith Mission workers there, and their ministries and needs.

Once a week, missionaries from different organisations visited and shared their work to amplify our knowledge and vision of what God was doing around the world. We also had School of the Bible lectures on Monday nights. These were open to public participation.

We generally had Saturdays off, and on Sundays, we visited local churches to observe different styles of churches and services, sometimes taking part. Occasionally, the whole college went away for the weekend.

When the week's practical ministry rota went up, we hurried to the notice board, curious about our next activity as they ranged from kids' clubs in local churches, open-air preaching in Edinburgh City Centre, visiting local estates for door-to-door work, and taking part in church services and ladies' meetings.

We also did six weeks of "summer work" with Faith Mission workers in different UK regions. This usually included missions and children and teens' camps.

"I watched you in college, marvelling. You were quietly strong, focused, deep, determined, accomplished, organised, efficient, effective, and powerful! You got so much done while I was figuring out where to start...!

You will always be Shigs, my little sister in the Lord, little only in that you are younger than me! I love you so much in Him, Shigs!"
- Hazel

The refiner's fire

Those years were a steep learning curve, best described as the Refiner's fire. I grew to know God's Word and the God of the Word and saw myself like never before.

Job 23:10 says, "When He has tested me, I shall come forth as gold." Gold is refined by a heating process in which the refiner removes the dross and impurities as they surface. This process continues until his reflection can be seen in the outcome. What a picture of us and God!

He sat by the fire of seven-fold heat,
As he watched by the precious ore,
And closer, he bent with a searching gaze
As he heated it more and more.
He knew he had ore that could stand the test
And he wanted the finest gold
To mould as a crown for the king to wear
Set with gems with a price untold
So he laid our gold in the burning fire
Tho we fain would have told him nay
And he watched the dross that we had not seen
And it melted and passed away
And the gold grew brighter and yet more bright
But our eyes were so dim with tears
We saw but the fire-not the master's hand
And questioned with anxious fears
Yet our gold shone out with a richer glow
As it mirrored a form above
That bent ore the fire, tho unseen by us

With a look of ineffable love
Can we think that it pleases his loving heart
To cause us a moment's pain
Ah, no! But he saw through the present cross
The bliss of eternal gain
So he waited there with a watchful eye
With a love that is strong and sure
And his gold did not suffer a bit more heat
Than was needed to make it pure[8].

I embarked on this process as God laid the foundations for future ministry. Shirley had to be made first, after which she could reach out to others.

The years weren't easy, but they left deep impressions on my life and changed me as God dealt with various issues in my life, one of which was fear. To find myself, I needed to be released from the fear I grew up with.

Psalm 34:4 says, *"I sought the Lord, and he heard me and delivered me from all my fears."*

I found wholeness and healing from my past in college. God filled me with his Spirit, and I became whole and free. I found the new me.

---

[8] PUBLIC DOMAIN

Prayer: An absolute priority

The greatest lesson I learned in college was that prayer was an essential tool in my ministry.

> *"It was at the Faith Mission Bible College in Edinburgh in the year 1997 that I first met my dear friend Shirley. Little did I know, when we shared Room 19, that a deep, precious friendship would develop, and Shirley or Shiggles, as we affectionately called her, would become like a sister! I have many memories of all sorts of escapades, but the most precious ones were our times of fellowship and prayer. God drew so close, and we experienced His power in tremendous ways. His presence was so tangible as we waited on Him in prayer and praise. Blessed days!"* —H

Through prayer, I realized the immense privilege, benefits and joys of knowing and waiting on God. I learned that hopeless and impossible situations could be changed through prayer. I also learned to move man through God by prayer alone.

> *"What a man is in his prayer closet is what he is. No Christian is greater than his prayer life, and his prayer life can be no greater than his personal life."*
> – Robert Murray McCheyne.

My walk with God is the heart of my life and ministry.

I formed lifelong habits at college that are now as essential as the air I breathe. I learned that God had called me to the ministry of prayer. There's much more, but he has specifically called and taught me so many lessons in prayer that I must lay hold of for life.

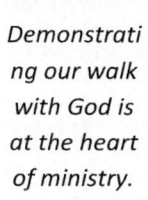

Demonstrating our walk with God is at the heart of ministry.

I don't feel fit to face the day if I haven't first met with God. Prayer, the heart of who I am, is my connection and key to abiding in God. I can't describe the immense joy and sheer privilege it is to sit at Jesus' feet. Whatever we do or attempt for God must be birthed and saturated in prayer; then, we can accomplish what we've already fought for and gained.

Remember, there's a work for Jesus that only YOU can do.

A group of us would meet at 4am to pray and battle for personal issues in one another's lives. We lost sleep, but the results made it worthwhile. The more prayer worked, the more inspired we were to continue.

God sometimes showed me friends and loved ones in pictures or dreams – both how they were and how to pray for them – and then I would learn from them that what I had seen was true. Such experiences were faith builders - how else could I know how my friends were doing without God revealing it? These real occurrences became foundations and habits I never wanted to lose.

During my first year, I became ill with chest pains and breathing difficulties, bringing frustrations to my study program. They were trying and difficult months but also times of great strengthening as I learned so much about the Lord and grew in him. During the months of being set aside, I was forced to slow down, and once again, God could speak to me clearly.

9th of May 1998

I wasn't well and my friends had gone on a college weekend away. I was on my own.

"Many years have passed since we shared a room together, but despite being thousands of miles and years apart, the bond has only deepened. God has moved us to pray for one another, often with no idea of their circumstances, despite living in different countries, cultures, time zones, and having different ministries. God is not bound by such. I do not know what the future holds, but we know Who holds the future.

I commit my dear friend to Him, trusting that we will continue to grow in grace and the knowledge of our Saviour."
- Hazel

I had a book, *The Street Children of Brazil*, by Sarah de Carvalho, which I had been too busy to sit down and read. Now that I was set aside, I started it. I had always been interested in Brazil and its various needs, and the book opened my eyes to a deeper challenge.

In one chapter, the author described a horrific scene entitled "the devil's playground", in which a gang raped a young girl so she could be accepted into the group. For the first time, what the street children go through hit me! Those streets were truly the devil's playground. He plays with these lives with only one intention - to destroy them (John 10:10[9]).

That afternoon, I began to sense a deep pull on my heart, just like back then for FMBC. God wanted to use my life to make a difference.

I was uneasy. Me? Go to Brazil?! It was too much to ask. I would never cope.

Surely, this was my imagination, I thought. *My heart was moved with compassion because of the need.*

One day, as I questioned these things, God spoke through that day's memory verse:

---

[9] The thief does not come except to steal, and to kill, and to destroy. I have come that they may have life, and that they may have *it* more abundantly.

> *"Also, I heard the voice of the Lord, saying, 'Whom shall I send, and who will go for us?' Then I said, 'Here am I; send me.'"* -Isaiah 6:8 (NKJV)

Was God asking me to go? This was a new idea to digest. The call to The Faith Mission was a challenge I had grown to accept, but now, Brazil? This was something else!

I needed time to consider this and seek God further. I was not ready to say, "Here I am, send me!"

But over time, the conviction grew. I was confirming this as his will. One year later (once again in May), I heard a sermon preached on the same text, accompanied by a clear sense that God wanted me to be a repairer of broken walls and restorer of streets with dwellings.

> *"The Lord will guide you always; he will satisfy your needs in a sun-scorched land."* - Isaiah 58:11-12 NIV

The conviction was clear. Shirley was to move out of her comfort zone and stretch to new heights in her walk with God. Having proved she could trust her heavenly father the first time, she obeyed, knowing he would meet her needs and carry her through EVERY challenge.

He had enabled me to leave my job, home, and family for the first time. With his help, I adapted to the college program.

God had drawn me aside during the time of illness to hear his voice and reveal the next steps on my missionary journey. Challenging yet exciting days!

I also realized the FMBC days were preparation for more. God was readying me for a far greater adventure and laying a foundation for a wider and deeper ministry than I'd ever imagined.

I was going to have to stand one day, a warrior in a land I didn't know.

> I counted dollars while God counted crosses, I counted gains while he counted losses. I counted my worth by the things put in store, he sized me up by the scars that I bore. I counted honours and I sought degrees, he counted the time that I'd spent on my knees. I never knew till one day by a grave, how vain are things we spend life to save[1].
> – *Author Unknown*

By my first summer placement a year later, I realized how much God had transformed this quiet, shy, foolish thing to be mightily used by him.

"Most assuredly, I say to you, unless a grain of wheat falls into the ground and dies, it remains alone, but if it dies, it produces much grain." - John 12:24

Broken things UCB
August 9th, 1998

Only when Gideon's army broke their pitchers could the light on the inside shine out.

Only when Mary's alabaster box was broken could its contents be poured out as an act of worship.

Only when the loaves and fish were broken could the hungry multitude be fed.

Are you getting the idea? We all need to be broken.[i]

Once again, the promise, *"I with you AM even to the very end of the age..."* (Matthew 28:20), kept me going at the end of the year.

Whatever I faced, God would NEVER leave me. The great I AM is with me until the very end.

Praise him for everything past and to come.

CHAPTER FOUR

READY FOR ANYTHING

After college, the first natural step before setting off to Brazil was to gain ministry experience and fulfil my commitment to The Faith Mission.

For two years, I worked with Aurelia, who became a friend, and other colleagues in the East Anglian, Yorkshire, and East Scottish district, with many adventures, lessons, experiences, and a foundation laid for Brazil.

Faith Mission life involved much change and flexibility. Ready For Anything (R.F.A.) was our motto and another tool that shaped my life. It meant adapting to various co-workers' personalities and ways of doing things, different church denominations, Christians, and groups of people, and being flexible in living situations, whether in caravans (often) or in people's homes.

God was continually refining, moulding, and preparing me. It wasn't usually easy, but I persevered and pushed forward step by step while leaving the results to God.

Caravan living was basic; parked beside the church or hall where we were working, it was our home for the period.

Showers and laundry were limited. We denied and humbled ourselves to depend on local Christians for provisions. These denials focused our attention on others and God's work instead of personal needs and desires (more essential lessons for later years on the mission field).

Each mission was three to four weeks long, and then it was goodbye and on to the next location, making life lonely. Maintaining friendships and establishing roots was difficult.

We lived by faith. Instead of a fixed salary, we survived on offerings from the mission and other donations. This new reality was another experience of God. I never went without, and while not always getting what I wanted, I never lacked what I needed, which built up faith to trust God in my finances, too. Whenever I put God first, he ALWAYS gave back to me.

One night, I sat at church in a dilemma. I needed to tithe, but I also needed petrol to get home. All from £10.

What should I do? The £10 went in the offering plate, leaving me with no petrol money. Immediately after the service, a lady approached me.

"I don't usually give you money," she said, looking flustered and embarrassed. "I feel strange doing so, but I believe God is prompting me to give you £10."

She handed it to me.

Wow! It was the exact amount I had needed and given to God. This experience has become the norm. Proving God in the little has allowed me to prove him with greater amounts of money, too.

God helped me prepare for numerous meetings and special events in various locations. We reached out to children, teens, adults, and the elderly through school assemblies, mothers and toddlers, ladies' meetings, Bible studies, men's breakfasts, old people's homes, camps, coffee mornings, community events, Great North Run, airshows, RAF army bases.

The Challenges were so great

The experiences and constant challenges gave me new skills and taught me to be capable through depending on God.

During one mission, our caravan was parked beside plot lands, and humanly, we yearned to pack up early and move on. The challenges were great.

> "It was a very small church that, looking back, felt like a tin hut. Our caravan was tucked in beside it, on a small piece of ground in an area like scrubland with unmade roads. At first, we didn't think twice about the location, but situations arose that made us increasingly nervous. Apparently, even the police only ever went there in pairs. But, surely, "go into all the world" included this dark and barren area? And if the Lord was with us, who could be against us? But we never quite knew what to expect.
>
> One day, on an unkempt little path to visit a house, we met a rather dubious character. He made strange threats about "coming to get us".
>
> Caravans, at best, are fairly flimsy affairs... but then there was an unexpected knock on the door. We were two young lasses with no backup plan or mobile phones (I don't believe they were around then). The nearest telephone box had been smashed, and we heard that folk involved with drugs were nearby. Shirley nervously opened the door, and I stood behind it, holding a frying pan in case it was the person who had threatened us earlier. Thankfully, it wasn't. What a relief! The mighty Lord always protected us, but it was a scary time."
> **Aurelia – co-worker**

Made In Brazil

Fear gripped us so often, but God protected and helped us overcome our fears and keep going.

During my first missions around Suffolk, God's presence was more intense and real than in other places. Lives were impacted, and marks were left that will count for eternity.

There was a palpable desire for God as people cried out with burdened, honest prayers. They recalled past stories of revivals and invited God to do it again. At times, God's presence was so tangible we sat silently instead of praying. At the same time, there was liberty to preach and share, with evidence of God's presence during the church services, as people responded. They made and left such imprints on us that we could no longer settle for less. We wanted to see more of this God revealing himself to his people. Even today, we and the church still remember these precious days. The following examples in this section are expressions of this.

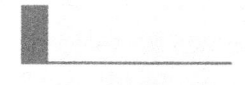

"He can only be your peace when he is your constant focus".

"As a sound dislodges an avalanche, so the prayer of faith sets in motion the power of God."

Within two weeks, three children accepted Christ at the holiday clubs, and a young lad also accepted Christ.

"I have been to Calvary' one young girl brokenly testified as she recommitted her life to God. "My burden is lifted."

During an evening service, another young man offered to serve God.

As Genesis 26:28 says, "We have certainly seen that the Lord is with you."

It was nothing we had done, just God. Wherever we went, we longed for that impact and for people to know it happened, not because of *us*, but because God was with us.

Of course, the unique experiences were closely connected to prayer.

Throughout the two years, God quietly continued to point me towards Brazil. As contented as I felt within The Faith Mission, it wasn't to be my resting place. It would be easy and logical to stay since the mission needed workers and the UK greatly needed the gospel, but God nudged me on. He wasn't going to let me remain in comfort. I had overcome challenge after challenge in the Faith Mission work and learned to serve and prepare in various settings. But this was only my preparation ground and ministry foundation.

The street kids of Brazil – Remember the eagle.

When I first felt called to FM, I questioned God. But his ways are amazingly perfect. He makes no mistakes.

FM's work was based on evangelism and preaching, while my focus had always been children and youth work. This was where my natural giftings lay, so why would God send me on mission work? Looking back, I needed FM to enlarge my boundaries, learn new skills, and ground myself in the Word. After developing in this area of ministry and abilities, God then turned things round and pointed me back to a youth and children's ministry - The street kids of Brazil.

If the eagle is never set free to fly, it will never reach its full potential. The mother eagle pushes her young out of the nest so they can discover how to fly and soar, which they would never learn in the nest. That said, the young mother doesn't leave them alone. She flies close, ready to swoop and catch them if needed.

If we are not gently pushed out of our comfort zone, we never soar or discover what it is to fly higher, know God's purposes and fulfil his greatest plans. Being pushed may be demanding, but it is God's supreme act of love to help us experience him in control, ready to catch and uphold us. Also, just as a ship was never built to remain in the harbour,

Ready For Anything

I had to trust him and set sail to follow his call wherever he was going to lead me in the vast sea of life.

God uses every means to draw our attention until we realize he, not our imagination, is speaking. Then, we step out in obedience.

I started hearing missionary reports. Some people went to work with street children in two organizations; a college lecturer shared his experiences in Brazil with me; another colleague's brother was out there. God was gently exposing and constantly drawing my attention to this country. I also heard sermons that challenged me.

In May 2000, a man spoke about how God can call us from one type of Christian work to another. Being in one type of Christian work doesn't mean we'll always remain there. I was serving in FM and could think,

I'm okay. I'm serving God, and he doesn't require more of me.

But he does – our obedience. He can move us from one Christian work to another, and we must go if he hasn't told us to stay. I began to count the cost. The price was high and the cross heavy, but God is worth more. Despite

> "Unless God specifically says stay, you have no choice but to go."
> - *George Verwer*

the cost, there would be no peace unless I went, nor would I enjoy his best without obedience.

Day after day throughout that month, God tugged on my heart using two Scripture verses:

"Go from your country, your people and your father's household to the land I will show you." Genesis 12:1 (NIV)

"And he who does not take his cross and follow after Me is not worthy of Me." Matthew 10:38

I repeatedly heard and read the words "GO" in Bible verses, in articles about God's call in the FM magazine, and on Church missionary pin boards.

On May 22nd 2000, it became apparent that my life had to be completely on the altar for God's blessing and fire to fall, but I was still holding back regarding Brazil, struggling to leave my country, family, and whole life behind.

As I listened to these songs, I finally gave in....

"I can hear my Savior calling... take thy cross and follow me....[10]"

I wanted to withhold nothing from Jesus, the lover of my soul.

---

[10] Where he leads me - Public Domain

That day, another landmark was reached during my personal time with God. I surrendered, knowing God's grace IS sufficient, and my Savior and Good Shepherd would carry me through.

I wanted to go higher and know more. I wanted to go up the mountain. The sacrifice needed to be complete so that I would not miss his very best for my life. And so here I was – ready to fly the nest once again, ready to leave my comfort zone, ready to give my Savior ALL that he was so worthy of.

I was petrified. Unknown territory lay ahead. But I wanted the best that my Good Shepherd had in store.

On May 28th, 2000, I nailed my colours to the mast and applied to UFM Worldwide. I had taken the first step. Once God reveals the next step, we have to take it.

In June 2001, I completed my final mission with FM in West Yorkshire with mixed feelings. FM had become part of me. I loved the work and fellowship and had been so grounded in a firm foundation. I had also grown immensely in my Christian life and walk with God.

There was more to discover; however, as God continued confirming his will through the Scriptures:

> *"For you shall go out with joy, and be led out with peace..."* - Isaiah 55:12

"Eye has not seen, nor ear heard, Nor have entered into the heart of man the things which God has prepared for those who love Him." - 1 Corinthians 2:9

"...because a great door for effective work has opened to me...." - 1 Corinthians 16:9

I could go anywhere in safety and confidence.

CHAPTER FIVE

STEPPING INTO THE UNKNOWN

June 2001

The heat! The humidity!

It was like stepping off the plane into a sauna on my first encounter with Brazil, the place to which God had called me. The only problem was that you couldn't leave this sauna when the heat got too much. It was permanent, and our bodies had to adjust. Even sitting in front of the computer brought on such a sweat. My body couldn't cope with handling things that took no effort, such was the heat.

I had met the others in the summer team at Heathrow, a team of us to be led by a UFM missionary.

There were many mixed feelings and emotions, fears and excitements. We just didn't know what to expect or how we would adapt together.

Yet again, God remains faithful – He NEVER fails, and he continued to comfort, to assure, to confirm.

Isaiah 43 – "You are mine...I have chosen you; I have called you..."

1 Corinthians 2:9 – "Eye has not seen, nor ear heard, Nor have entered into the heart of man, the things which God has prepared for those who love Him."

Despite the unknown territory, God had called me. His presence would go with me.

Praise God. I'd never met the team before, but I wasn't going alone. As we drove away from the airport, I looked out of the car window and observed extreme poverty that shook me to the core.

Later, I lay in bed listening to the competing noises from the dogs, people, music, frogs, and cockerels. How would I cope? This wasn't a visit before heading back home to stay. I would soon return permanently. Fear and doubts resurfaced. Could I cope with this and stick to it for the long term? My friends and I stuck out like sore thumbs, and people knew we were better off.

Like a banana being peeled, all my props were removed until I had nothing to lean on, nothing secure or familiar, just God and me. It's easy to trust God in our comfort zone where we know the ropes and can survive by being independent and self-reliant, but when we are plunged in at the deep end, know no one, when the food is strange in a new culture and different climate, where we cannot speak or communicate, we are out of our depth and must learn what it means to fully trust and prove God's faithfulness.

We visited various places where we observed the work with street kids and other missionaries working in churches and river villages.

The experience was an eye-opener with challenges and many new things to learn and adapt to. People were happy and content with very little and yet ready to give so much to us. Life started early in the morning because it was cooler, which took some adjusting to.

Some places didn't have running water, so we bathed in the back yard using barrels of water.

Life was generally laid back and slower-paced, probably due to the heat. I learned an important lesson that served me when I returned later to live in Brazil - to slow down my pace. In the UK, my days were crammed with nonstop activity, so the slower days in Brazil took patience, to begin with. Events started one to two hours later than scheduled, and no one thought anything of it.

What did this teach me spiritually? A lesson from Mary and Martha (Luke 10).

Martha was concerned and pre-occupied with many things, but Mary chose to sit at Jesus' feet and listen, something that can be challenging but necessary in our often-busy task-driven lives.

Within six weeks, I gained a completely new perspective on life, returning to England with much to consider and digest. This was to become my future home and life – a very exciting but daunting prospect!

16th September 2003

I set foot in Brazil for the second time under the umbrella of UFM Worldwide, this time knowing it was home until God told me otherwise, once again experiencing the new situations I faced in 2001 and many more. The simple things of life were no longer straightforward.

For instance, washing dishes using a cold-water tap meant putting the washing-up liquid on the sponge instead of filling the sink with water. Toilet paper was not flushed away but placed in a basket at the side. Some houses didn't even have a toilet, just a hole in the ground outside! That took some getting used to!

Stepping into the Unknown

It was like having to relearn life all over again, with the language being the greatest challenge. Until you can speak the language, the barriers are huge, and communication is limited.

Food shopping took such effort. Knowing what you wanted, working out what it was called in Portuguese, and then locating it in the supermarket was tricky. Then there were all the new foods you had never seen before, and having no clue how to prepare or eat them. Money was another challenge. Recognizing new coins and working out exchange rates to calculate whether items were expensive or not. It was all very humbling. I was no longer independent and needed help to function in the smallest of things.

Imagine being unable to visit the doctor because you couldn't explain the symptoms or then understand the diagnosis.

The missionaries could not drive over there until our license was translated, so it was back to life on the bus. But what a terrifying experience! You hardly knew your way around the city, and there was no language to confirm that you were on the right bus or make sure you got off at the right stop. The buses were overcrowded, and people were squashed in like sardines, often hanging off the steps to hitch a ride.

How our trust in God changed. We were hopeless and helpless and totally reliant upon him.

When I eventually collected my license, I learned to drive on the left and on the other side of the road. To top it all, huge traffic jams and congestion were the norm. Ah! Why wasn't life straight forward?

The daily heat was intense and draining, and that didn't change with time. You had to find a coping mechanism to deal with the baking heat, thunderstorms, floodings and power cuts, most of which were normal during the rainy season. Power cuts meant no water, leading to more survival lessons on coping without water in hot, sticky temperatures!

Then there were the mosquitos. How they loved and bit our new blood in those first months!

Other pleasant experiences were just as different, like birthday parties. The Brazilians love a good party and any excuse for cake. Unlike the UK, so much effort and decoration went into their huge birthday cakes, and the enormous slices were *not* good for the figure!

I will never forget my first experience after church one night. A lady from the church asked if I would like a piece of cake.

Stepping into the Unknown

"Yes, please!" I replied. To my shock, she served me a huge slice that would easily feed four or five people! I had to somehow try and eat it by myself!

And so, amid enormous lifestyle changes and great transitions, of which these are a few, I started my new life as a missionary in Belem, a city with a population of approximately 1,392,031 in the north of Brazil, close to the mouth of the Amazon.

To begin with, I lived at the MICEB[11] campus, our mission base, studying Portuguese four mornings a week with a local teacher. The fifth morning, I worked in the girls' home at the children's project, where I was exposed to other Brazilians, their cultures and ways of life. I practised what I was learning, beginning to input into the project where I would later work full-time.

The project opened in 1996 to provide aid and recuperation to children and teenagers on the streets of Belem and from other at-risk situations. When I arrived, we primarily worked with teenage girls, but the work has since developed.

---

[11]Missão Cristã Evangélica do Brasil

In 2004, as I was finishing my 9 months of language study, the project bought land in another town outside Belem and built a new home for boys aged under 12.

I started my fulltime work within the project there, cooking the way the Brazilians did, handwashing my clothes and taking afternoon siestas. Life was a constant learning curve, and caring for the children's health, education, etc., was very demanding. From my experience of the local hospitals and general extreme needs, it was obvious that life was not easy for these people.

The early mornings (5:30-6:00) were a huge challenge. I had to develop new habits while persevering to maintain my own walk with God during it all.

"My deepest prayer, my highest goal is that I may be like Jesus.[12]"

Despite all this, my heart's desire was to work on the streets in Brazil. I sensed this call while reading Sarah de Carvalho's book that referred to the streets as the devil's playground. I was thrilled to see this realized in 2005 when the project

My deepest prayer, my highest goal, that I may be like Jesus.

---

[12]Hymn - I have one deep supreme desire (Public Domain)

Stepping into the Unknown

bought a building in downtown Belem, and I was on the new street team.

Working on the streets opened our eyes to the extremes people go to – some were forced to live like this, while others chose this life. Glue sniffing, drugs, and prostitution were the norm. Food was either stolen or begged for, people bathed and washed their clothes in the river, canal, or sewers. They usually moved about in groups or gangs, with a leader whose rules or demands the others conformed to.

> *"We went out onto the streets at night to evangelise. Sometimes, the kids rejected the food we offered for 'better' alternatives from other religious groups like the Catholics or Spiritists who were trying to reach them on the streets. Some visits led us out of Belem, going the extra mile to do a complete work, e.g. crossing the river to Bacarena to take a child to live with her family there or taking two adults to recuperation centres outside of Belem. We amplified our work and went beyond the normal work of the project."* - Luis

The suffering was real and deep; vicious cycles of addictions and poverty kept the people bound and unable to escape. It was a huge task to see these lives change. We had to gain their trust through years of patience and perseverance while developing effective strategies to work with them. There were setbacks and disappointments, but also joys and success stories, as you will see further ahead in this book.

And so, this became my new life. My life was never the same, and my perspective changed forever.

CHAPTER SIX

HOLDING FAST TO THE CALL

God's Kingdom call is to reach out with his compassion to the lost to bring his message of peace, forgiveness, and hope.

How I wanted to answer this call and proclaim salvation in Jesus' name. Yet this would be no easy task.

"The devil tries to uproot people from where God plants them. If he can get you out, he has been successful, but if you do not budge, even during great conflict, you spoil his plans." – Author unknown.

I obeyed the call, but that call was repeatedly tested, leading to one of the biggest lessons ministry taught me: Perseverance.

The trials and difficulties were constant and unceasing. We came through one situation and heaved a sigh of relief, only for the next problem to emerge. The interminable challenges ranged from practical problems, e.g. blocked bank cards and car problems, to greater issues involving relationship problems and huge spiritual battles.

> *"The devil tries to uproot people from where God plants them... if you do not budge, even during great conflict, you spoil his plans."*
> – **Author Unknown**

In this continuous learning curve, the more we encountered and faced, the more we learned about ourselves and God.

The loneliness in my first years

I had friends and people who were good to me, but close friends who knew me and whom I trusted were another continent away. I needed to find strength and comfort in God, but spending time with him became a massive endeavour, resulting in a soul wilderness experience.

With the language difficulties, I couldn't understand most of the church services, either. I became a piece of coal that had lost its heat away from the fire.

Deuteronomy 8:2[13] soon became real to me. I remembered that the Israelites' 40-year desert journey

---

[13] Remember how the Lord your God led you all the way in the wilderness these forty years, to humble and test you in order to know what was in your heart, whether or not you would keep his commands.

allowed God to humble and test them, know what was in their hearts and whether they would keep his commandments.

I searched my heart. *What did I want?*

And the answer came to me in a flash. Only him! God was all I wanted and needed (even now). The tough times drew me closer to him.

As the hymn says... *"Yet in the hardness God gives to you, chances of proving that you are true."*[14]

The tests were opportunities to prove my character.

God puts us in uncomfortable crucibles, not to destroy, but to mature, refine and strengthen us. Once again, Shirley was being made. Like Daniel, I learned to maintain my Christian character no matter what came against me. Daniel went through the fiery trials that God permitted, and God was with him throughout.

A new challenge

God also promises to "restore our souls" (Psalm 23:3).

Over the years, I experienced the beautiful healing that comes after the storm and pain is past. Yet the difficulties seemed never-ending. In 2005, things were extremely tough. Underlying problems and personality differences

---

[14] Keep on Believing – A hymn by Lucy Booth. Public Domain

Made In Brazil

came to a head at the project, resulting in a separation of personnel.

Several of us were burnt out and needed respite. The pressure was so intense that we were no longer coping, just surviving, but we learned to let go and move on, love, accept, and forgive. We saw God's grace through it all, teaching us to be more like him with the difficult people in our lives. Loving when it is the hardest makes us more into his image. It was practical Christianity.

With these changes came a new challenge. I wasn't simply to work on the streets team. I was now leading it!

I felt inexperienced and inadequate in many ways: for the work, as a young girl leading men, and as a foreigner leading Brazilians.

Another intense challenge and steep learning curve, to which God helped me adjust by giving me a love for the work and those we served and the perseverance and passion to empower and transform their lives. This kept me pressing on with the energy to go further in the middle of tremendous battles and dangers on the streets. Life was exhausting.

The project encountered financial problems, placing us under tremendous pressure and limiting certain aspects of our plans. By 2006, I was ready to leave, telling myself it

Holding Fast to the Call

would be easier to return to the Faith Mission in the UK, where life was straightforward and serving God was a real joy. Brazil was too difficult. Too intense, with no let-up.

Once again, I was reminded that these uncomfortable crucibles would mature and refine us. It was part of the process!

Part of Christian maturity involves processing pain, enabling us to grow in our understanding of him. The process teaches us to work out our faith in life's grey areas, where we need clarity, so we can work life out.

My purpose remained clear, and that clarity helped me press on, even during desperate times. Admittedly, I swayed sometimes, but God repeatedly confirmed the call to see street kids' lives restored.

> *God whispers in our pleasure but shouts at us through our pain."*
> *– C.S. Lewis*

> *"If we are obedient to God, have sought him, and he is not speaking... he is probably saying, 'stay right where you are, don't change a thing.'"*

I was not to quit. The devil didn't want us touching and impacting the lives he was destroying, but God wanted us here! There was, perhaps, an even greater work before us.

There was no way we were to quit. God had much more for the street kids of Belem.

> "But may the God of all grace... after you have suffered a while, perfect, establish, strengthen and settle you."
> 1 Peter 5:10

Thankfully, we witnessed this as God brought us through the personnel and financial crisis, reestablished the project and settled the different issues. 2008 saw the project with new leadership, a new outlook, and strategies.

> *"It was during the early days of being responsible for the project. We were all learning on the job. I had recently taken on bookkeeping and financial responsibilities for the first time in my life and was figuring out how to do the job in Portuguese and reais, as well as how to suit Brazilian law! We could not pay the workers for two months and were unlikely to do so for the third. The main funding came from UK supporters, so the exchange rates (which were not favourable) impacted how much Reais we received.*
>
> *One morning, the team prayed about the situation and for the workers who fulfilled their responsibilities without pay or complaint. That afternoon, one of our UK missionaries on the team phoned to say that someone had deposited money into their UK bank*

account for the project work. S also called with a similar story, meaning we could pay all that was outstanding to the workers. Is God good, or is God VERY good?!

The day before I was due to deliver the payments, I arrived on my street to find several people outside my home. Apparently, a man had tried to break into my house but left after the neighbours shouted at him. I opened the two padlocks and my double-locked heavy front wooden door. The guy had actually entered my home!

I rushed into the bedroom, panicking because the money was in my wardrobe. The floor was covered with my clothes, and the wall was marked with dusty footprints. The burglar had removed some roof tiles, kicked in the ceiling to access the bedroom, and then left the way he entered before my arrival. My heart sank. The money must have been stolen, I thought, looking into the wardrobe. Right in the drawer were my passport, plastic card wallet and a bright orange envelope containing the money! The man opened and emptied the wardrobe but missed othe important items at the back of the drawer.

I felt a distinct slap on my wrist and heard the words, "Have more faith, M". The following day, I paid the workers as planned, telling everyone of God's wonderful act of kindness.

> With 28 children in three homes, a street team and nearly 20 workers, the project spent much time living "hand-to-mouth", but God provides, even in very tough times. We experienced times of little cash, with each governing body member having plenty of ideas of how it should be spent and what was necessary/important. There was not much agreement, but the Lord sorted it all out. We began receiving food deliveries, enabling us to spend money elsewhere. The foodstuff included cabbages, oranges, yoghurts and fish heads, but there was always enough for the homes and our neighbours. Many, many people were blessed.
> **– Mo, Missionary colleague**

Job worshipped through his suffering. He lost all, yet he bowed to worship his God. I have learnt that praise is intrinsic to pushing back the devil and lifting the spirit of heaviness. No matter what we are going through or feeling, God is worthy of our praise and worship.

> "We had a saying in the project: "Only eternity is forever". Whatever anyone was going through on any one day would eventually come to an end.
>
> One area this did not and does not apply to is the friendship that God brought to S, K, and me. I believe the friendship was made in heaven and will last until eternity. I am the same age as their parents, and yet,

the difficulties we experienced together, the support we gave each other, and the Holy Spirit's work in us have resulted in a wonderful relationship. K now lives in Canada, S in the north of England, and I in the Midlands. We have not worked together since 2013, but our friendship has not grown cold. We holidayed together in 2014, and meeting at Toronto airport felt like we had been together the day before. We meet regularly through Zoom and WhatsApp these days and are never lost for words, questions, and prayer requests. I look at them and think how 'crazy' it all is, but I am so grateful to God for His grace and guiding."
— **Mo, a missionary friend**

The devil's attempts to remove us from the work were constant and subtle. There were distractions and other tactics, yet God gave the victory, no matter how intense the testing. God wanted me here; I was not to be removed!

In October 2007, I hit another crisis. The toil, difficulties and trials had become overwhelming, and I felt battered, bruised, injured and weary. I had nothing more to give and no strength to go on, yet I didn't want to abandon the assignment. I knew I could never turn back. I had to be faithful to my calling and continue to run the race.

Perseverance was key!

Made In Brazil

God gives the Holy Spirit (the *Parakletos*[iii][15]) to come alongside and help us across the finishing line. He is there to comfort, enable, and strengthen us until the end.

> *"I was not disobedient to the heavenly vision."*
> —Acts 26:19

> *"Be thou my vision, O Lord of my heart,*
> *Naught be all else to me save that thou art*[16]*."*

At home in the UK, over Christmas 2007 and New Year 2008, God clearly gave me fresh hope and direction from his word again.

> *"You did not choose me, but I chose you and appointed you that you should go and bear fruit and that your fruit should remain...."* John 15:16

I was chosen and appointed for God's purposes and plans. There was NO turning back!

---

[15] in the widest sense, a helper, succourer, aider, assistant - of the Holy Spirit destined to take the place of Christ with the apostles (after his ascension to the Father), to lead them to a deeper knowledge of the gospel truth, and give them divine strength needed to enable them to undergo trials and persecutions on behalf of the divine kingdom.
[16] Be thou my Vision, hymn

"One thing I do, forgetting those things which are behind and reaching forward to those things which are ahead. I press towards the goal for the prize of the upward call of God in Christ Jesus."
Philippians 3:13-14

CHAPTER SEVEN

ADVENTURES AND CHALLENGES

It was another typical day on the streets. We were out searching for an angry young woman whose children had been removed from their domestic at-risk situation (living on the streets). We approached her, knowing it would not be easy. After all, we were in her territory, and the streets were dangerous. She marched towards us, and we apprehensively continued in her direction. Her fury was palpable. Suddenly, it was as though she melted right before us. Her angry demeanour broke, and she began to tremble and cry.

> *"There was such a shining light behind you, and I knew God was with you. I couldn't touch you."*

"I was so angry with you," She said when we reached her side. "I intended to harm you, but I just couldn't.

Adventures and Challenges

There was such a shining light behind you, and I knew God was with you. I couldn't touch you."

I have never forgotten that moment. What a testament to God's faithfulness and protection. I saw her change so dramatically and had to believe she truly saw something over us. God not only protected us, but he showed her it was him. This incident impacted her and us until today. We may be in vulnerable and dangerous locations, but we are not alone. God gives us the confidence and courage to face dangerous situations. He who called us will enable us to do the work and bring the treasures out of the darkness. It is not what happens to us that matters but what God is doing in us.

In this chapter, I thought I would share certain experiences, adventures, and challenges to give you a picture of the reality we lived with. Some are funny, others more serious, but all demonstrate God's hand and protection over our lives.

Life in Brazil can be violent, and assaults are common, especially against foreigners. People assume we are rich and have money. We had to be careful, wise and alert in all situations to avoid putting ourselves in unnecessary danger.

In 2004, I received a puppy rescued from the streets (she was a faithful friend through the years, often protecting us).

One night, at about 4 am, we awoke to continued barking. There were some men outside our home. Thankfully, the dogs scared them off, and nothing further happened to us. We later discovered that our neighbours had been burgled.

In 2007, I accompanied one of our teenagers to the hospital. I was at the counter booking his appointment when we heard gunshots coming from the bank inside the hospital. The receptionist hurriedly ushered us into her office. When everything quietened down, we inched our way down the stairs.

"Quick! Take cover!" Someone bellowed. One gunman had fled into the hospital.

I ran to the nearest shelter, which happened to be the toilets, and a few of us squeezed into the cubicles. Shortly afterwards, a hospital worker suggested we take

"I remember going in and out of that area, a red zone so dangerous, where even the police feared to tread, yet we went in under God's protection. A was caught up in a street situation with a new-born baby and we tried to accompany and help him in a little bedsit he had found. Going in there was always a challenge for me, knowing the intensity of the danger, yet we ventured on in to help this couple." L – one of the men who worked with me on the streets.

shelter in his office, as it was safer. We were locked in there for more than an hour. Eventually, we were told the armed man hadn't been found, but there was sufficient police presence so we could run out through the police shield to the hospital gates.

Because my colleague was waiting for me and we'd had no contact so far, I had to run for it. Thankfully, to safety!

Our type of work can be dangerous.

We have had several adventures out on the streets, too. On one occasion, we needed a police escort to remove two children from their drunken father. And then there was the married couple in dispute over their six-month-old son. We had worked with them for some time. The father was recuperating with the project but the mother was still on the streets. Their son, whenever he was not with his mother on the streets, was cared for by her friend.

We were helping the father get custody so the baby would no longer be at risk. We sat with them in the drop-in centre and negotiated what we thought was a peaceful solution. However, on reaching the car, the woman jumped on the car and started screaming, accusing me of kidnapping her son.

Initially, the onlookers around the car seemed to believe her. They stopped the car as she continued making a huge scene, claiming she didn't know me. Despite our best efforts, the whole thing got out of control. There was a huge traffic jam and general chaos. Someone took my car keys and called the media and the police, who escorted us to the nearest police station. The woman denied knowing me despite my having worked with her for so long. Thankfully, the baby's father defended me, and the full story unfolded. However, rather than resolve the situation, the police returned the baby to the mother, who went straight back onto the streets. Our efforts had been in vain. Ah, the struggles of the work! The extreme circumstances restricted our ability to follow the case through, and we could only encourage the father to fight the case alone. But without support, he was weak and reluctant to do so.

At one stage in our ministry, we regularly visited two sisters in prison. Two of us usually went in, and we were accustomed to undergoing a body search before we entered. One Sunday, I went in alone, only to discover that the rules had been tightened recently, and I was to be strip searched. Ah, the embarrassment and humiliation!

As we contemplated and joked about it afterwards, we acknowledged that serving the Lord and reaching these girls required our willingness, and we couldn't stop the visits because of this development. We went along the following

Adventures and Challenges

week, dreading but counting the cost of continuing our ministry. Surprisingly, the previous week had been a one-off! What a relief! The event became a long-standing joke: missionaries doing the Full Monty (giving your all) for Jesus!

Then there were the cultural challenges. Once, I was on the shift on my own at the girls' home when the leader drove in with a kombi full of live chickens.

"Shirley, these were donated,' he said. 'You need to kill and freeze them today!"

"WHAT?!" I shrieked.

We were grateful for all donations, but how would I cope with this one? Especially considering my example in leading the girls.

"Can we not keep them until Tia S's shift?" I asked.

"No, it needs to be today."

Clueless as to even how to go about this task, I was relieved when he killed ten chickens right before my eyes, leaving us to pluck and cut them. Thankfully, one of the girls knew what she was doing and set us all to work. I will never forget that afternoon. Although I now know how to pluck a chicken, I hope to never have to do it again!

Natalia (not her real name) is a girl we have worked with over the years but have never seen fully get off the streets because of a strong drug addiction and knowing little other than drugs and street life. In 2005, I wondered if taking her into our own home would make a difference. We could give her individual attention, and she wouldn't be pressured by the strict routines and the other girls in the project home. Maybe she would cope better going at her own pace and ability.

I took her home, and she lasted six days of intense spiritual battles. I have recognized over the years that in working to rescue souls from the devil's territory and transform their lives for Christ, we engage in real battles.

I will never forget that week. On the Tuesday, a motorbike hit me right outside the girls' home.

Although I was not at fault, the man took advantage of my being a foreigner and took me to court for a claim that took two years to resolve. Of course, this was another wearying distraction and an added pressure we didn't need.

The afternoon of the accident was spent at the police station, sorting out paperwork, which stopped me from caring for this girl.

The following day, we decided to visit the shopping centre, which had never felt risky compared to some dangerous areas where we worked. I was in for a shock. As

Adventures and Challenges

we went to get some food, gunshots rang out, and chaos erupted, with people running and screaming.

The streetwise Natalia's initial reaction was, "Tia, give me your cell phone!" and she stuffed it down her knickers!

We ran into Burger King's kitchen and hid behind the bins until things calmed down. The next day, I became extremely ill, and my friend had to take care of Natalia. However, Natalia threatened my friend with a piece of glass and ran away. The sickness lasted several days.

The stress and battles were intense, and this was just one life of many we were trying to reach.

"At a time, we weren't going out because one of us was always sick, and it wasn't wise for two to go out alone. God made Shirley realise we needed to stop and listen to what he had to tell us. This marked my life. Our work was the type that never stopped, and God had to force us to stop so he can speak to us (many in today's churches are in the same position). This situation made a deep impression on my working on the streets with Shirley." L – my work colleague on the streets.

Other stories

Life was certainly never dull. One afternoon, as the thunderstorm outside worsened, I called the girls inside to prevent them from being hit by lightning. I went to shut the back bedroom windows as the rain was blowing in, only to somehow be hit by a bolt/electric current. What an awful sensation! I stumbled back to the living room, where a neighbour helped me recover. I lost the feeling in one of my hands for several hours.

Another day, on my way to church, I had to drive across two wooden bridges over small rivers. Fear gripped my heart, knowing the bridges weakened over time. That night, I knew the bridge was bad, but it was the only route to the church. Suddenly, there was a loud crack! followed by a bump! The car had not made it onto the planks, and the wheel fell into the hole of the bridge.

What a nightmare!

Some young men were lifting other cars out, and they soon had me out, but, too shaken to continue driving, I asked them to take the car safely over to the other side. You can imagine my terror the next time I had to attend that church. Yet, this fear had to be confronted and overcome. I couldn't stop going to the church for fear of crossing a bridge!

Thankfully, there were delightful adventures.... like

- a herd of monkeys passing over our heads in the trees above during our team meeting.

- Accompanying a summer team from the UK to Manaus and swimming with dolphins as they swam underneath, prodding our feet and pushing us upwards. What an awesome sensation!

Missionary life isn't all challenges. There are real joys and exciting new experiences.

We once went to share the Good News in the river communities and visited a little church up a creek. The congregation arrived and parked their canoes underneath the church before entering barefooted. I was asked to give my testimony. It was awesome and impactful to share about Jesus Christ in a tiny corner of the Amazon.

God leads us where he wants and uses us as he wills.

CHAPTER EIGHT

LIVES WE HAVE TOUCHED

Throughout our ministry, we have touched hundreds of lives, both on the streets and in the project homes. I thought it would be good to share some (disappointing and success) stories to show what God has done and is doing. No matter the outcome, we trust him to fulfil his purposes and remain his instruments to impact these lives. Working alongside them and seeing God at work has deeply touched us, too.

Sometimes, we have been overwhelmed by so many needs, not knowing where to start. For example, a girl arrives at the home, or we meet her on the streets; then we conduct a family visit and discover significant needs there, too.

It is essential to be continually sensitive to God and his leading to know what he would have us do in each situation. We can't change them all, but we can make a difference for some. As the story below reminds us:

Lives we have Touched

> *A young boy was walking along the beach. The tide had washed up hundreds of starfish, and they were stranded on the sand. One after another, the boy picked up and threw the starfish back into the water.*
>
> *A man walking past stopped to observe what the boy was doing.*
>
> *"What's the point," he asked after watching the boy for a few moments. "There are so many of them. You won't really make much difference."*
>
> *"But I made a difference for this one," The boy replied, throwing another one back in. "And I made a difference for this one...."*
>
> *And he continued putting one in after another*[iii]*.*

The moral of the story is that each life matters. We need that perspective in a work that would otherwise overwhelm us.

In 2006, I met Maycon (not his real name) in one of the key groups we used to visit on the streets. He was around 18 at the time. In August 2007, he started rapidly losing weight and becoming weak. During one visit, he could hardly sit up, so we rushed him to the local accident and emergency, but they wouldn't accept him because he was a street kid with no documentation. He needed urgent medical help, so we involved our social worker, found him another hospital further away, and he received a drip and temporary care. It took her a month of fighting the case before she got him a place at the city hospital.

Meanwhile, a men's recuperation centre was willing to take him in until we resolved the situation. All the while, we tried to get further information concerning Maycon's family, but he was unwilling to share much with us. He had been on the streets since he was eight years old, with little contact with his family. It was such hard

"I was 56 when I arrived in Brazil, having had little contact with children. I feared and felt uncomfortable with them, even after God clearly instructed me to go and work with this street children project! Fear was hard to overcome, but I had opportunities to know the boys and girls better and, over time, saw them as real heroes and heroines.

They had come from tremendously difficult backgrounds, suffered so much physical, sexual, and emotional pain with no spiritual experience to help them. Yet, many of them eventually forgave their abusers and wanted to rebuild their family relationships.

It takes two to make a relationship and they didn't all succeed, but the change that made them want to try and the Holy Spirit working in them greatly encouraged us all."
– Mo, a missionary colleague

Lives we have Touched

work to convince him to reveal any information, but he eventually opened up.

The social worker and I found his cousins (his mum had disappeared years earlier). We tried unsuccessfully to locate his identity documents. Despite knowing the gravity of his sickness, no one visited or even contacted him. Some (not all) street kids are completely on their own, surviving life with no support. Maycon refused to reveal his family circumstances to avoid being reminded of the extent of his suffering.

Healthcare is still basic here. Each patient normally has someone to accompany them, but the project workload and round-the-clock care in the homes meant that no one had sufficient time or energy to do this task, and Maycon could not stay alone. Eventually, someone from the recuperation centre agreed to stay with Maycon during the daytime, and I stayed with him at night. This experience was exhausting and emotional. It also opened our eyes to the needs within the hospital.

At this point, Maycon entered the hospital, literally dying and unable to eat. The attendants did little, and his care was left to us, with no medical experience. They brought him biscuits on his first day.

"He can't even eat," I explained. "He needs liquid or a drip."

"He'll just have to wait until teatime, then," replied the attendant.

I was horrified!

Maycon lay in the hospital corridor for several days before he got a bed. Other people sat waiting in chairs, but thankfully, the staff recognized that Maycon was too weak to sit up and supplied the trolley.

He was subsequently diagnosed with TB and taken to an isolation room containing only his bed. I slept sitting against the wall in the corridor until a nurse finally gave me some cardboard to lie on and a privacy screen.

"Auntie, it's the wrong way round," Maycon commented to me one day. "I'm in the bed, and you're on the cardboard like a street kid!" His eyes filled with tears. "I now know how much you love me since you're willing to do this."

I realized his need afresh, but also that I instinctively wanted to care for this lad when no one else would. What a profound impact this would have on him.

During this period, God spoke to me a lot about self-sacrificing, unceasing, unconditional love and the fact that it is practical love that wins people to him. They see us as real and willing to go the extra mile, not just taking them a snack and chatting to them on the streets. Maycon soon came to understand God's love and accept Christ.

In Galatians 4:19, Paul mentions labouring until we see Christ formed in people. It is intense labour, but oh so worth it when they accept Christ, that after suffering on earth, they will be free from all suffering in eternity.

Maycon was transferred to a specialist hospital in October for another month before being released back to the men's recuperation centre.

I returned to the UK on home leave, not realizing I would never see Maycon again. He died on the 12th of February 2008. Wanting to return to the streets, he ran away from the recuperation centre to die amongst those he considered his "family". Thankfully, the Lord took him from his pain and suffering.

Shortly before, he told some of our coworkers, "You showed me what real love is. It is God's love."

Praise God for his changed life.

Our biggest desire is to see Christ formed in the street kids and to find them present in eternity as we worship together before his throne. In September 2005, God impressed on me deeply that our work is about having them

Made In Brazil

in heaven with us someday. The conditions in which we find them on the streets do not glorify God, so our goal is to see them rescued from the devil's destruction and restored to the praise of God's glory.

There was another 19-year-old lad in the group (I will call him Carlos). I counselled the younger group members with the green bag[17], but Carlos kept asking to participate. Eventually, I gave in and was deeply moved by his gratitude for the opportunity to talk, share, and express his emotional needs. He came to understand that God valued his life.

Carlos was seriously attacked, ending up in intensive care, where we visited and shared his need for Christ. It was the last time we saw him. He didn't return to the streets, but we lost contact. This was a shorter relationship, but we believe a difference was made.

Patricia (not her real name) is one of our success stories. When she arrived at the girls' home, I was assigned as her key worker. She was addicted to drugs, her brother had been murdered, and she was now an only child, but her mother was distraught as Patricia's drugs were destroying their

---

[17] The **Green Bag is an exclusive tool developed by Lifeword's Pavement Project that** utilises images to broach and address problems children and teenagers face through games, Bible stories, and interactive conversations. For more information, visit https://latinamerica.lifewords.global/pt/home-pt/

family. We did a weekly Bible study, and she started taking English lessons, hoping to travel to England with us someday. Despite her best efforts, she had many ups and downs and setbacks.

When she was around 18, Patricia seemed to reestablish herself. She returned home and kept in contact with us, but the contact lessened over time until 2011 when we discovered that she had learnt to drive, taken a hairdressing course, and was now at university studying law.

She bought a small area of land and built a small house for her family, and was now able to pay for her own visit to England. It was such a joy seeing her dream fulfilled in 2011 when Patricia shared her testimony and story with several churches and supporters. In 2012, we were privileged to attend her wedding.

We first got to know Vanessa (not her real name), aged 15, when she turned up at the girls' home from a background of significant family problems, having lived in other government homes. For her first Christmas, she asked for a doll and a box of chocolates.

I was stunned. *A doll at 15!*

Then she explained that she had never received either. It was wonderful to fulfil such a simple dream.

We got to know Vanessa well over the years and worked closely with her family, who were in poor conditions with many children. One Christmas, Vanessa expressed her longing for a mum who loved her. Many of these kids have never experienced the sense of belonging to a family that loves and cares for them.

We visited her mum with her. It was painful to witness her mother's direct rejection and hatred firsthand. We had to work on teaching Vanessa to forgive. It is easy to say, but faced with what she went through, it took a lot for her to forgive. I'll never forget the day she felt up to it. I accompanied her and witnessed the awkwardness as she stumbled over her words. But she released forgiveness to her mum and listened as we shared God's love for her. Her mum subsequently died in 2010. We keep trusting that Vanessa's testimony made an impact.

She left the home when she turned 18 but kept contact. She worked with a local family and attended church with me. Then she started saving her salary to fulfil her dream of attending Bible college, but sadly, for various reasons, she would leave or be dismissed from her jobs, many of which were live-in. We wondered if she found each environment stressful and needed her own space, so we experimented by paying for her to rent her own little bedsit and begin an independent life, working during the day and studying at night. With the money saved, she bought some necessities for her home in a lovely, safe part of town, loved and supported by Christians from her church.

Vanessa eventually moved to another state, where she got married and has lived to this day. In doing what we felt God wanted for her, we touched her life, and the seeds of the gospel were planted. We must trust God now to protect her and continue the work.

God promises much to us, and we hold on to those promises....

> *"Those who sow in tears WILL reap in joy"*
> (Psalm 126:5).
>
> *"Let us not become weary in doing good, for at the proper time we will reap a harvest if we do not give up."* (Galatians 6:9 NIV).

Thaisa (not her real name) was another young woman we helped because she had a baby girl with her on the streets. We met her and her "husband" at the drop-in centre. During that time, they came off the streets and rented a little room.

Since Thaisa wanted our help, we went there for a weekly Bible study and took food donations. They did well and remained off the streets despite their challenges and drug addictions. They also had two more children within a short period.

Our support was not just to get them off the streets but to be "whole" through restoration, recuperation, and healing. One area in which Thaisa needed healing was the relationship with her parents. Her mother lived with Thaisa's twelve-year-old son, whom she had abandoned, and her father lived in another area with her older daughter, who was seven at the time.

Thaisa's father did not believe the changes were real or lasting and didn't want anything to do with her. Her mother was more open and even offered some land behind her house to build and live there with the little ones.

Our project helped them build a small house, and we continued with the Bible studies. As a friendship formed with the whole family, we presented the gospel to her mum and won Thaisa's son's confidence. We also counselled his needs from being abandoned by Thaisa. It was a real joy to witness their complete reconciliation and a privilege to bring the whole family true healing and hope.

Thaisa had her setbacks and weaknesses (her partner died from certain illnesses he had picked up on the streets), but she made slow progress in general. The children started school and learned fast. They attended church with us, and we held evangelistic meetings in their home. One year, our UK summer team re-floored their house and reached out to their neighbours through various children's activities and sharing Bible stories on the streets.

Unfortunately, Thaisa eventually abandoned everything and disappeared. We still don't know where she is, which is a typical setback and disappointment with our work. However, her children have grown and found hope and life, with a sense of joy, togetherness and belonging. The rest of the family has remained firm. They continue happily with life, and we still maintain links with them.

The last story I want to share is that of another couple we met through the drop-in Centre.

Guilherme (not his real name) was a simple, sincere young lad who kept asking us for help. It can be hard to judge each person's motives and distinguish who is genuine from someone wanting to use us. We finally visited where he lived to see what he wanted.

Guilherme had rented a small room for himself and his pregnant partner (I will call her Katia) to avoid her having the baby on the streets. He asked us for nothing and wanted reassurance that we would support them. We started weekly visits and sought to read and pray with them. Guilherme's room was always immaculate despite being in the poorest and most dangerous area of Belem. What little they had, they cared for.

When the baby arrived, they had no idea how to look after her, and she became malnourished. Concerned, we accompanied them to the nearest hospital with a special unit for malnourished children, another eye-opener in my ministry. I never realized the unit existed, and the children's needs and desperation were so distressing.

Guilherme's family required continued support to care for their baby, and as we got to know the extended family, we discovered that Katia's grandmother looked after several sick and malnourished grandchildren. Thankfully, we got one of them admitted to the same unit, and the child was restored to full health and strength. Guilherme's mother eventually agreed to care for the baby, who is now being raised by her grandmother and is doing well. Guilherme worked hard collecting and selling plastics for recycling, the proceeds of which went to his mother as child support. Since he and Katia could not read or write, we gave them lessons at the drop-in Centre.

Katia became pregnant again, this time with a boy, but her life was not stable. She and Guilherme eventually split up, and she began using drugs and slowly drifted back into street life. She wanted to take the baby with her, but Guilherme fought to bring up his son.

The consequences of street life subsequently caught up with Guilherme, and his health deteriorated so rapidly that he was brought to live in the project to receive support and good nutrition. With the right treatment and care, his health picked up, and we returned to counselling. We worked with and taught him to read and write. We witnessed much development across his life, including the first time he read a word from the Bible and wrote his name. He prayed simply and believed God for his baby son's welfare. His heart's desire was to share how God transformed his life with those among whom he once lived. He visited his mother, daughter, and family, seeking to reach them for Christ through organising evangelistic meetings in his home.

In February 2009, at the age of 30, Guilherme started school for the first time and made steady progress. Then, on September 27th, 2009, he was baptized. What an impacting experience! It was the first baptism since I had been working on the streets. Knowing Guilherme from when he slept huddled on a piece of cardboard on a dirty back street to witnessing the triumphant moment of his baptism was a joy and privilege!

Sadly, in 2011, his health deteriorated again, and we sensed his time was coming. He had fought the good fight, but his body could no longer continue. We prepared to lose him, but he seemed to be at peace and ready. The last days came quickly. On December 2nd, 2011, Guilherme passed into glory, a transformed life that had left a deep imprint on everyone and was now enjoying God in eternity. Guilherme had been genuine, and he challenged us with his simplicity as we saw God take him from sin and destruction into eternal glory. It was an awesome privilege to witness God's restoration and Guilherme's transformation.

There are many setbacks and disappointments, but these testimonies make the whole work worthwhile and worth going on.

If we make a difference just for one, our labour is not in vain. We continue to press on to see all God intends for these precious lives.

CHAPTER NINE

GOD SETS THE SOLITARY IN FAMILIES

"Well, what do you think? Do you want to put your name forward or not?" Our leader asked me during the meeting.

I was stunned. I had prayed and pondered this for years, but now the judge was making the decision, I didn't feel ready for this commitment.

Before I arrived in Brazil, God gave me a dream to be married, foster and adopt children with no family, and run a farm or project to further help restore their lives. I always sensed that my time in the project was an initial, temporary step until God made the way to fulfil my dreams.

When I started working at the girls' home and was still learning the language, I met seven-year-old Barbara (not her real name). She was behind with her schooling, so I taught her numbers and colours, which helped improve my Portuguese. Our relationship grew, and I loved teaching her.

In July 2004, the project leader told me Barbara couldn't return home because of her circumstances.

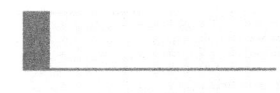

'Would you consider adopting her?' She asked.

> "God sets the solitary in families"
> Psalm 68:6.

There was no way I could consider that at the time. I was adapting to a new country, and I was single. Barbara would be better off with a married couple. But the seed was planted, and it niggled at me.

Was this something I should consider later? In addition, several of the children needed families; how would you choose one and not another?

I prayed, considered the matter, and closely watched as Barbara's situation developed. In July 2005, I attended a month-long course with another project that also worked with street children and children at risk in Belo Horizonte. The course focused on preparing for this type of ministry with practical experience. It was very beneficial, and I learned so much.

One of the seminars examined adoption in light of God adopting us as his children and placing the solitary in families. Each one of us needs to know we belong.

Once again, the thoughts gripped my heart, but I sensed the vision's timing was not yet right. Like Mary in Luke 2:19, I kept and pondered those things in my heart.

Barbara later returned to live with some family members, and we remained in contact. Then, a phone call came through to the project office on May 13th, 2009. Moments later, the leader came into the room.

"Guess what? Social Services are bringing Barbara back to the project!"

At this point, the questions started again.

Does God want me to adopt Barbara after all this time? Here she is, back in my life without my having done anything.

The leaders within the project prayed to discern God's intentions.

During a court hearing, the judge pronounced that he was going to remove Barbara's parents' rights. She was up for adoption, and he gave the project thirty days for suggestions.

This was when our leader asked me: "Well, what do you think? Do you want to put your name forward?"

Despite my doubts and fears, this felt right. I couldn't deny the way God brought her back into my life. Not knowing what the future held, I stepped out in faith and trusted God to lead the way. The judge agreed, and in Nov 2009, Barbara moved in with me. I was still at the project, and we gradually adapted to each other within the project's protection and environment. Life changed dramatically.

In Dec 2010, I received her official temporary guardianship certificate. I was a mother and still maintained my responsibilities within the project with God's enablement. Once again, we were on the steep learning curve of being moulded into what God intended.

On 8th October 2005, I received my permanent Brazilian visa through an effortless natural process.

"Shirley, you're meant to be staying here," my coworker joked. "This is God's place for you, and he has confirmed it by giving you your permanent visa."

His words were so true. God had much more for me here, and this was only the start. He was going to fulfil my dreams and desires.

> "Eye has not seen, nor ear heard, nor have entered into the heart of man the things which God has prepared for those who love Him." – 1 Corinthians 2:9

As I mentioned earlier, we went through difficult times within the project, throughout which God continually reminded me not to lose sight of the vision. It was for an appointed time, but it would surely come (Habakkuk 2:3). As I kept trusting him, it became clear that these kids mostly needed a family unit where they belonged, with the intense work being reaching and seeing them restored. The words *Rescuing Hope* began to unfold within my heart.

> *"My soul, wait silently for God alone, for my expectation is from Him."* Psalm 62:5.

These kids needed hope restored within them to believe in the possibility of change and transformation. We would provide them with a family unit and work with them and their families to see complete restoration all round. It also felt right for this new project to have strong links with a local church.

From June 2007 onwards, this vision intensified, and God repeatedly confirmed in his word that I was to advance, go up and possess the land.

It was time for a change.

I also sensed that I had to 'step out of the boat' to 'walk on water'. It was time to leave the project and step out in faith to see this vision fulfilled. I also had a strong desire to settle down and establish a family unit of my own into which I could bring others.

Made In Brazil

I had met Felipe (not his real name), a young Brazilian lad who had joined the work at the boys' home at the start of my years in Brazil. We worked the same shifts,

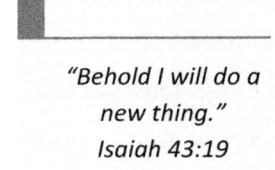

"Behold I will do a new thing."
Isaiah 43:19

and a natural friendship developed between us. We worked well as a team. When I started the street work, we didn't see each other as much, but he was later moved across to work with us. Our friendship grew to the point where we became engaged. However, we later called it off and went down separate paths.

Was he the one?

At the end of 2007, I left the project and returned to England for a break and time of Home Assignment[18] with questions and struggles going through my mind and heart. The recent months within the project had been very tough, and I was worn down with other personal battles and issues. The ministry-related spiritual warfare was real.

After a period of counselling, I was encouraged to dream afresh and place my aspirations before God again. I vividly

---

[18] I worked a cycle of two years in Brazil and six months in the UK on Home Assignment to rest, spend time with family and connect with supporting churches and individuals, where I reported back on my ministry in Brazil.

remember sitting on the rocks at Portrush Beach, and as I did exactly that, faith, hope, and peace began to rise in my heart, and I knew God would fulfil my deepest desires. My soul was being restored.

That was such a time of blessing.

God personally revived and restored my soul with his healing. A promise came from Isaiah 43:19, with the assurance of a fresh start.

"Behold, I will do a new thing."

Renewed and refreshed, I returned to Brazil in August 2008 feeling like a new person, with freedom, fresh faith, and a vision for *Rescuing Hope*.

I attended the language school in Campinas for a Portuguese refresher course, where I experienced another landmark in my ministry. I went to Rio de Janeiro to visit the Pavement Project with a group from our project and the UK. I had already done their training and was using the green bag for counselling sessions.

"I was not disobedient to the heavenly vision."
- Acts 26:19

During this visit, they asked me to become the green bag facilitator for northern Brazil. I was thrilled and honoured.

A promotion ceremony later took place in their little office—God was enlarging my territory and expanding my ministry.

The church I attended in Campinas had a mission focus that reawakened and challenged me afresh to the needs around me. I decided to be more involved in evangelism and church ministry.

A couple of years later, God brought me and Felipe back together. In November 2010, we revisited the Pavement Project and renewed our engagement on the beach.

A new era of life and ministry in Brazil

Felipe was now pastoring a small congregation in the interior, and things would be different after we got married, which was another ministry expansion and fulfilment of God's prompting me to be more involved in church work and evangelism.

I started helping out and generally finding my feet at Felipe's church. The ladies there welcomed me with open arms, and their acceptance and attitudes made the transition smooth.

Felipe and I started dreaming about *Rescuing Hope* again and began looking for a suitable property.

Without knowing about my desire to write a book, Felipe also challenged me to do so. It felt like God was about to allow me to slow down and fulfil this dream, too.

So many changes happened all at once with ministry, marriage and Barbara's guardianship. Humanly, it probably looked crazy, but God continually assured me that it was his plan and his way and that his favour surrounded me like a shield, fulfilling his purposes and working it all out.

2011 was the start of a new era

"BEHOLD, I WILL DO A NEW THING!" Isaiah 43:19

We believed God was not only doing a new thing but a big thing!

Felipe and I settled into married life with a teenage daughter and church ministry, looking towards all God had for us as a family and fulfilling his plan for *Rescuing Hope* as a family unit, reaching those on the streets and providing opportunities to be set in a family, be restored, and transformed.

CHAPTER TEN

RESCUING HOPE

It was our day off. We had driven out to the beach, where I loved to walk the dogs, relax, wind down, and reflect on life. After wandering along the beach, we sat down to rest and chat.

We were discussing where to live after the wedding. It was time to start Rescuing Hope, but we needed somewhere to live, so we began praying for God to lead us to a property suitable to live in and develop for Rescuing Hope.

Not long after, we were blessed to find an ideal property up for rent in a small town outside Belem. It was a condominium located on a main street near the girls' home, with privacy since it was walled and plenty of space inside and out for future development. We decided to rent it as our main residence and then a smaller house at the back that could be renovated for the girls to live in.

Six or seven months into our marriage, we started caring for two-year-old Thalia (not her real name), the little sister of Vanessa (whom I mentioned earlier). Having moved away from the project, Vanessa was not only living independently, but she also took sole responsibility for her sister's upbringing after their mother died. Vanessa had to work to support them financially, so we offered to look after Thalia from Tuesday to Saturday. Vanessa worked weekdays and spent weekends with her sister, which worked well. Thalia was great company for Barbara, and she became a part of our little family, and we were quite attached to her.

A year later, Felipe and I began to volunteer one day a week with the street team and soon felt stirred to move forward with Rescuing Hope. Ana, a girl we knew well, returned with her 18-month-old baby after some time away from the project. But, the project could not legally take her in because she was an adult. However, with a baby involved, we realised their situation suited our vision for Rescuing Hope. Was this God stirring us to action?

Then, the mission offered to buy the property. If the owner agreed, that would be confirmation that we should take Ana in. It was a real step of faith as we felt that continuing to pay the high rent to him was not a wise investment, but would he sell? However, the sale was agreed

Made In Brazil

upon within two weeks. Surely, God had done great things for us.

Ana and her baby moved in with us, and a dear friend from church, who was a builder, agreed to renovate the back house for them. The dream to bring girls into our home as part of a family had begun, with all it signified – love and security while learning future life skills. Each one needed a secure family unit to deal with their past and damaged emotions and move forward. Rescuing Hope was a God-given vision, but I did not realize how much it would cost personally. But, as said earlier, making a difference in one life is worth it.

Alongside these good things, other events were happening in our lives.

Just after we started looking after Thalia (before Rescuing Hope opened), I became pregnant, much to our joy and excitement, which was dashed by a miscarriage at 12 weeks. When I was in the hospital, I experienced God's peace and presence in a precious way, from being upheld by God's people and surrounded by his loving care as people carried me through with all their messages of care, comfort, and support. There were questions, but there was a deep-rooted peace through faith in God. God had given, and he had taken away. He knew why, and we had to trust. I had such faith,

Rescuing Hope

believing in God's promises that we would yet have children. This gave me the grace and comfort to move on. God had written the days of this baby; they were determined, ordained, and written in his book. When we couldn't understand, when we couldn't trace his hand, we could trust his heart.

The more I pushed into God, the more real he was. Our busyness drove us on, and life just continued to unfold.

That same year, I became the UFM coordinator, which involved caring for the other UFM missionaries and responsibilities with MICEB. This also involved some travelling, and I had the joy and privilege of seeing other ministries and expanding my own awareness of what God was doing here in Brazil.

The end of 2013 involved another trip away. This time to visit Vanessa, who had now married and moved with Thalia to the south of Brazil. I wanted to meet her baby son and, of course, see how she and Thalia were doing. It was so lovely to see the fruit of working with them and witness everything God was doing.

Vanessa was concerned about her younger brother Lucas, who was living in the Belem area with her elderly grandmother. She really wanted him to live with her since her grandmother didn't have much time left to live, and he didn't have much other family support.

On our return, Felipe and I offered to help Lucas move down south, and he could live at Rescuing Hope until then. So, the work of Rescuing Hope continued to grow. Again, not exactly in the way we had planned or intended, but God brought each life to us at the right time, in his time and in his way. Our role was to care for and love each one: a great responsibility before God and yet a great joy, just like Lucas brought to our home. He just seemed to fit in so naturally. It was a new dynamic having a little boy around, and it was good for Barbara to have a 'little brother'. Lucas was a real charmer who won everyone's hearts and fitted so well into our work in the church.

Amanda was the last girl we took in to live with us. She wasn't from the streets but the daughter of a family in the church. She had got involved with drugs, and the family were at their wits end with her. Maybe some time away from the Vila and these influences would be just what she needed. She agreed to come.

Each of these kids brought their own personalities and dynamics to our home. It was a delight to be able to work alongside them so specifically and really be able to minister to them as we lived family life together. They took part in our daily routine and got involved in church life and times with the kids from the project. We worked closely to counsel, advise, and help them appropriately with personal issues and problems, as well as help them continue their academic education. We firmly believed God had brought and entrusted each one into our hands. This was an awesome responsibility and yet such a great privilege, too. They blessed our home tremendously, and we had great times and real joy watching them triumph and gain several victories. As iron sharpens iron, handling the challenges presented through their circumstances and behaviours made us grow.

Over the years, Barbara's behaviour also became extremely demanding, which shook my faith to the core. I had to fully depend on God to show grace and unconditional love. Much prayer! In response, I felt God telling me to die to self so that she might live. "Unless a grain of wheat falls to the ground and dies, it cannot produce fruit" – John 12:24.

Much more could be said, but in summary, I came to understand what it meant to be "made" and pruned, often asking myself, "What would Jesus do?" and doing likewise, even when it went against my natural responses. It was painful and difficult and probably one of my greatest challenges, but years later, I am seeing the fruit and reward of perseverance.

Shirley was still being moulded as we continually depended on the Lord for wisdom and the right approach to various situations.

CHAPTER ELEVEN

"GRINGA" IN THE INTERIOR

We passed over the wooden bridge, careful to keep the car on the parallel planks. A small barrier on each side overlooked what the Brazilians call an "*igarape*", a small area of natural water among the jungle of trees. A kilometre-long main road with small colourful houses stretched ahead, and a huge Brazil nut tree loomed high above, a landmark as you entered the *Vila* (village). A short way ahead, some churches, a snack bar, a bakery, and smaller bars.

"A gringa (foreigner)?!" A stuck up snob. How would she fit in? She wouldn't last among us!

Before meeting Sister Shirley, I wondered, "Would she be cool or boring?"

My first impression was that she was snobbish and conceited with her nose in the air. But I was completely and utterly mistaken!"

In the middle of the Vila was what they call the *praça*, the village square, where the small school, a tiny children's playpark, the catholic church and a central football field were all located. Across the road was the community centre for local social events and small sandy tracks leading to more houses behind the main road, totalling 200 houses. In the centre of this rural Vila, 18km from the nearest town, was the little Baptist Congregation where we would now be based.

The ladies had preconceived ideas of a foreigner based on appearance, and this one didn't fit their judgment! Twelve years later, as I returned to the UK, they pleaded and cried, *"You belong here, stay here! Go bring your parents to live here!"*

As they became my family and the Vila my home, I saw once again how perfect God's ways are. I fitted in so well, and their simplicity suited me perfectly. I loved their freedom, laid-back attitudes, close-knit community, sense of belonging, joy, contentedness, and generosity. There was much to learn.

The abundant natural resources included varieties of fruit, Brazil nuts, the occasional meat someone had hunted, freshly caught fish and that day's bread, and access to the nearby farm where we obtained milk from the cow to make yoghurt and butter. Even though buses only ran once an hour, everyone looked out for one another, and the drivers helped take shopping and supplies back and forth.

I flourished. The change was so refreshing after the hustle and bustle of cities like Belem. The climate was just that bit cooler, which helped physically too. Despite adapting to ministry in a new context – church-based work instead of the children's project – and Brazilian church ministry, for that matter, it was like receiving wings to fully utilise my gifts and abilities while working as the pastor's wife.

The small congregation consisted of a group of committed ladies, a few men, several children and young people. I immediately rose to the challenge, beginning with the teenagers. The work soon had about 20 regular attendees, and we later set up a Sunday afternoon children's club. I loved both ministries and felt so much joy and blessings as they developed.

With the other demands of church life, our prayers were answered as husbands also committed to coming regularly, and we soon had a small group of faithful men.

The congregation accepted us with open arms and became our extended family, providing everything from fun and fellowship to practical help. There were challenges, as usual, but it was generally a real blessing with much encouragement.

I implemented the green bag ministry at the church, and one of the ladies was trained to carry it on in future.

Since we wanted to expand the church's vision to focus outwards instead of on their own reality, we promoted missional opportunities during the services and to the youth group, eventually organizing a mission trip. Felipe and I were thrilled to take two women and two teenage girls to a town in Maranhão, where we visited various groups of Guajajara Indians.

It was a new adventure for us all.

The six of us piled into our car, and Felipe and I took turns driving for four hours each before swapping. Neither of us had done a 17-hour journey before. The road stretched endlessly before us, going up and down through a barren wilderness. The conversation soon died out, and the passengers at the back fell asleep.

Suddenly, there was a loud "BANG!" and everyone jerked upright.

"What happened?" One of the ladies asked.

After Felipe pulled over on the steep downhill incline, we stepped out of the car.

The tyre had burst!

Felipe tried changing it, but he couldn't manage it alone.

"Gringa" in the Interior

What now? We were in the middle of nowhere.

One of the ladies and I decided to find help on foot. The day was hot, and the road stretched before us with nothing else in sight. With no other option, away we went. Thankfully, we located a local garage, and someone from there fixed the tyre, so we were soon back on the road.

This delayed our timing, and since other missionaries advised us not to cross the Indian terrain at night, we found somewhere to stay and continued on our way the following day.

"When Shirley recommended that I take my first mission trip, I experienced a mixture of fear, anxiety, excitement, and uncertainty. But during the trip, God challenged me about missionary work, and I also started taking my relationship with him more seriously. It was the best choice I ever made.

One thing that caught my attention the most was the culture and language. Despite being Brazilians, the indigenous people had a totally different view of the world from what I was used to. They also had their own language, which was new and interesting. The first word I learned in Guajajara was "Katu", which generally emphasises something good but can be used

> *in different situations. The linguistic issue is quite extraordinary.*
>
> *Their reality was also a turning point for me. In Brazil, we are free to share Christ, yet many people don't know Jesus. There are people longing to hear the gospel, which was what I found in the Guajajara - people who really wanted to know Jesus. As we passed each village, I felt more burdened, but what could I do? Nothing! But God began to give me the desire to dedicate my life to cross-cultural missions. That was how I decided to fulfil the 'Go' of Jesus. Of course, I needed preparation, discipling, and to let God work first in me and then through me."*
>
> —Adriane – one of the young girls we took with us.

We were all amazed at the Indians' desire for biblical teaching. They kept asking us to come back and teach them further, opening our eyes to the immense need and inspiring my heart to reach the unreached.

At a women's conference a few months earlier, as the speaker shared how she was called to work with Indians, I sensed that we weren't to put our roots down too firmly as we would probably be moving again. Considering how many times God had stirred my heart – often long before the thing actually happened – I knew this would also become a reality. I surrendered to God, deciding to be available and free to move as he led.

Adriane's story

"Shortly before this trip, Shirley mentioned the Word of Life Missionary Institute North (IMPV), but I wanted to prioritize my academic life. However, after the trip to the village, I started considering this possibility as a great opportunity for spiritual growth, and to acquire tools that would help me in the propagation of the gospel.

But then new challenges arose. No one from my family or church had financial resources to send me to the Biblical Institute and the monthly fees were well out of my reach. Getting the resources seemed impossible, but "We know that all things work together for good for those who love God, for those who are called according to his purpose" (Romans 8:28).

The Lord opened the doors using someone from another country, who didn't know me, but had heard about my desire to prepare for the mission field. The person blessed the beginning of my ministry, and I was able to join the Bible training."

—Adriane

Some months later, during a mission-focused church service, Adriane, one of the young girls who went on the Guajajara trip, responded to God's call. While she was singing a song with the chorus "I will go", the lyrics convicted and changed her. We have since had the joy of watching her go on to fulfil that call after training for full-time service. Neither her family nor the church had the financial conditions to send her, but God wonderfully provided the whole year's fees in one gift.

Her conviction and calling remained firm, and she graduated from Bible School and continued her training with New Tribes Mission to work with indigenous tribes. She has since returned to work with the tribe we initially visited!

Adriane's story continued...

"Several other people were a blessing during my training, and I am very grateful to each of them.

It's amazing how God accomplishes all things. Through a missions trip, he helped me understand that His plans were better than mine, and a life satisfied in and working for him is infinitely better than satisfying and working for my own selfish desires.

Today God has used me among the indigenous peoples, not because I deserve it, but because of his love, grace, and mercy in Jesus Christ. With that same love, I desire to reach the lost, "… that at the name of Jesus every knee should bow, of those in heaven, and of those on earth, and of those under the earth, [11] and that every tongue should confess that Jesus Christ is Lord, to the glory of God the Father.." (Philippians 2:10,11)."

—Adriane

"Gringa" in the Interior

What a blessing and fruit from a simple idea to focus on missions and look outward. Other saints have been inspired and stimulated by seeing God raise other people to serve him. An elder and his wife later took over the church leadership, and a young girl, Aline, trained to work with children and took that over. (See her testimony in Chapter Thirteen). An older lady who could not read and write also allowed me to teach her.

Although we often struggled to understand why God gave us so many responsibilities in so many areas all at once, we saw him weaving new possibilities together as our ministries interlinked. From the fun days with the church youth together with the girls from the project, a lady from the church realised a personal dream by going to work at the project. She had been unemployed and wanted to work with teenagers, which she fulfilled and much more. It was a job, ministry and calling.

We organized a second mission trip with the same group, and this time, two men and two children joined us to work with the Indian pastor.

We immersed ourselves in the tribal culture, staying with a Guajajara tribe for three days, where the ladies held a children's holiday club, and the men accompanied the Indian pastor on home visits.

This was another learning curve as we strengthened our relationships, shared fellowship within the team, and had enjoyable adventures.

The summer of 2013 saw the beginning of a new work after two ladies started attending our church from a town across the river.

We took a UFM summer team from the UK there and hosted a children's holiday Bible club in the local library. Others from the church helped out, developing further skills, opportunities, and fellowship. We were greatly encouraged within our own church because of the summer team's visit.

In August, a lady and two teenagers were baptized.

In September, as UFM coordinator, I travelled to Manacaparu, a town in the Amazon, to visit missionary friends who were ministering up there. My heart was deeply stirred, and the burden reawakened for the 300 unreached Amazon tribes.

> *"And so I have made it my aim to preach the gospel, not where Christ was named, lest I should build on another man's foundation."* Romans 15:20

I had surrendered myself to be a dart that always hit the Lord's goal. Now, my nest was being unsettled again, and God was preparing my heart for something new.

Back home, I shared all this with Felipe. It felt like we were being moved on to new things and a freshness in ministry. We considered the New Tribes Mission course and other links, which only confirmed our thoughts.

> *"To preach the gospel in the regions beyond you...."*
> —2 Corinthians 10:16

Our ministry continued to expand and be blessed, yet the parallel battles and trials were becoming deeper, more intense and more painful.

CHAPTER TWELVE

THE VALLEY OF THE SHADOW OF DEATH

As 2014 began, I looked back over 2013 and could only describe it with the word PAIN.

On February 13th, 2013, I became pregnant again. Over the next few days, I experienced such excruciating pains that I had to stop whatever I was doing until they passed. This happened on three occasions, the third being so bad that Felipe rushed me to the hospital. However, we were given no clear diagnosis and told to return for a routine ultrasound in four days.

Sometime that night, on my way to the kitchen, I experienced a pain so sharp and unbearable that I passed out instantly. I have no idea how long I lay on the floor, but when I came round, I was in such agony that I started shouting for Felipe, but he was fast asleep. I somehow dragged myself to the sofa and lay there in cold sweats, unable to do anything

The Valley of the Shadow of Death

but cope with the pain. Feeling desperate for the toilet, I crawled to the bathroom, still trying to get Felipe's attention. I began to go in and out of consciousness.

When I came around again, I kept weakly calling for Felipe, to no avail and finally got his attention by banging on the wall. He carried me back to the sofa, where I drifted in and out of consciousness while he went for help.

Thankfully, a UFM missionary friend was working at the girls' home nearby. Felipe brought her over, and they lifted me into the car and drove to the hospital. All the while, I kept lapsing in and out of consciousness.

The hospital care was disappointing. Firstly, they would not attend to me because I was unconscious and couldn't tell them my symptoms. Finally, they conducted various tests to confirm the pregnancy. The baby was fine, but I had appendicitis.

From 2am until 6pm that evening, I lay in the accident and emergency area. The pain became so agonising that my body convulsed uncontrollably, and I kept crying out.

Later that evening, they finally took me for an ultrasound (before the operation to remove my appendix). However, the doctor told Felipe that I was haemorrhaging. Apparently, it was an ectopic pregnancy that had burst, and I had been haemorrhaging for 22 hours.

He also told Felipe that I only had hours left to live unless they acted immediately. I can only imagine what Felipe went through, especially as he wisely didn't share the information with me so that I wouldn't panic.

I still had to wait until around 11 pm before the surgery. The whole time, a song from Psalm 23 that we learned at church kept going through my mind.

> "Yea, though I walk through the valley
> of the shadow of death,
> I will fear no evil;
> For You *are* with me."

That night was a miracle. I had no idea how close to death I was, but God's presence and comfort were so real, and looking back, I can testify that God had my heart prepared and resting in him. Today, I can praise him, knowing I had literally passed through the valley of the shadow of death, and he was right there looking after me. God preserved my life because my time wasn't up yet. I am also grateful to Felipe for pulling out the stops to keep me from death.

The Valley of the Shadow of Death

After the operation, I was still in agony. There was no relief, and I couldn't sit or move. Getting to the bathroom alone was impossible. Yet, the hospital discharged me that day.

We had no chance to deal with losing the baby as we had to find the care I needed to recuperate. A lady from church agreed to live with us for two to four weeks since I was fit for nothing. My only memories of that time involve pain. I couldn't sleep, relax, or sit up. It was awful feeling so helpless and reliant on Felipe and Adriana for absolutely everything. They were long, long days, and I became homesick, bored, and frustrated with my limitations. I couldn't even cry because of the pain.

It took five days before I could sleep, and only after my friends came around and prayed for me. Meanwhile, God spoke clearly through the following verses;

> *"This sickness is not onto death, but for the glory of God, that the Son of God may be glorified through it."* John 11:4

> *"And his name, through faith in his name, has made this man strong, whom you see and know, yes the faith which comes through him, has given him this perfect soundness in the presence of you all"* Acts 3:16

After that good night's sleep, it became a running joke that I was so happy just because I had slept! I appreciated little things and was grateful for each achievement as God restored me to physical normality.

I learned some valuable lessons in those days. I grew to understand the suffering the Brazilian people experience through a lack of adequate health care and would be more sympathetic, understanding, and helpful to those in similar situations. I also witnessed a miracle as God spared my life from the shadow of death, which he obviously did for a purpose, giving me a fresh incentive to maximise every opportunity to share Christ with others. I was ready to die, but what about the many who were not ready for that moment? We never know when it could take us by surprise.

I also gained a special friend in Adriana, who helped me in those most difficult days when my family was on the other side of the world. I am grateful for her selfless care and to her husband for allowing her to stay with me.

More problems

Before my physical normality was restored, a new whirlwind of problems arose with Barbara, and I struggled to cope. I was so emotionally affected that I didn't deal with losing my baby until several years later. It felt like fighting to

The Valley of the Shadow of Death

survive, yet we knew Barbara was meant to be with us. God wanted to do a **complete** work in her life.

There were so many questions in my mind – Why, why? The word I remember God saying is "I AM."

It was a month before I could leave the house, and then life became a rollercoaster, with so much happening. Our ministry was richly blessed with much fruit, and Felipe and I seemed to grow stronger in prayer and spiritually. But there was little time to truly process all that had happened.

So many times, God uses the circumstances and situations that generate so many of our whys as means for him to be seen in our lives.
– Shirley

We were eventually able to take a holiday in June, during which the word continually coming to sum up every area of our ministry was "Restoration". We felt God wanted us to focus on those in desperate need of restoration and rebuilding, whether in our home, at the project, or at church.

CHAPTER THIRTEEN

THEIR STORIES TOLD

Patricia (not her real name) – 36yrs old

"For He shall give His angels charge over you, to keep you in all your ways." Psalm 91:11

"In 2003, I had the worst experience of my life and walked away from the Lord at 16 years old. I had lost my only brother so tragically and got involved with bad friends, who offered me drugs that I accepted, thinking it would lessen my suffering, but I sank into a pit of mud and depression. My mother was already struggling with my brother's loss, and she suffered even more after my addiction.

God sends angels to help you!

One day, I felt God telling me to stop and return to His arms, but I didn't have the strength to fight the addiction. I was 17 years old and had suffered for a year, but God assured me that he would be with me if I accepted help. My mother sought help from Social Services, and I was sent to a children's home. Then, some missionaries took me to the girls' home, where I met five angels – Shirley, Lynne, Kelly, L, and Mo - women committed to rescuing lives like mine with God's help.

I would be lying if I said it was easy, but by God's grace, I became free from drug addiction.

Shirley studied the Bible with me, and during each study, I reflected on God's great love for me. I threw myself at his feet in prayer and won the victory over addiction. God restores and makes us new as we surrender into his hands and accept the help that he sends.

Today, I am a lawyer, businesswoman, wife, and mother of two children.

NOTHING is impossible with God – Patricia

Carolina (not her real name) – 67 years old

"I came from Belem, bought a piece of land and lived with Thaisa when she was twelve. She became pregnant and gave birth to Marcelo at fourteen. With no one to help me, I went out to work to sustain her while she stayed home.

One day, she went away, and then just as suddenly, she came back six years later.

"Mum, I don't want this type of life anymore." She said, "I want to live with you and take care of my son."

But five months later, she met a lad outside our house and Laura (not her real name) was born. At this point, Thaisa's dad helped out as I was then unemployed (although I later found a job where I left home at 7 am and returned at 8 pm). My house was covered with plastic, so I worked in Sao Caetano for a month to earn some money for the roof tiles while Thaisa stayed at home. Eventually, she left to live on the streets again.

She returned with three more children and asked for a bit of the land behind my house. Apparently, the children were living in a creche in Belem, and Thaisa asked to bring them to my home every weekend. The weekend pickups made me late for work, so I offered to have the three children living with me.

We struggled at that point, but then I met Shirley and Felipe through Thaisa. Shirley brought us food, and Felipe helped us construct a new house, so five of us were not sleeping in one double bed. I can only thank God today. He also sent assistance through other missionaries like Auntie Mo. With God's help, Shirley and I fought for the children.

Socorro is now 18, Marcelo, 28, Maria, 17, and Fernando,[19] 16. Laura lives with my ex-husband and her aunties in Belem. We went through many tough battles (only God knows the extent), but Shirley always brought food hampers and made sure the children lacked nothing.

Battles

At one point, I fell ill, but God strengthened me and got me back on my feet so I could keep the children on track. Socorro studied events management. Maria is in her 1st year, and Fernando is in his 2nd. Thank God that I can do something for them, which is to help them study. Auntie Shirley was like a godmother to us, an angel that the Lord put in our lives. She is part of our family, and I pray God always protects and blesses her.

My daughter abandoned her children with me, but I don't feel guilty as God knows my heart's desire to have her with me. She doesn't even know she has two beautiful grandchildren, Deborah and Ronaldo[20]. I don't know where I went wrong with Thaisa, where she is today, or if she is even alive, but I believe I will see her before I go to be

---

[19] Not their real names.
[20] Not their real names.

with God. I hope she is ok. God knows all things, and I have given my children and grandchildren over to him.

I am thankful for my house, where I and the children have our own rooms, and for my health, without which I could not continue raising these children.

Shirley was and will always be special to us. I ask God every night to illuminate her paths and bless her in all areas of her life. I believe God will give her much happiness and that her dreams will be realised, in Jesus' name.

Amen!"

Ana – 29 years old.

In 1999 and 2000, it was common to see children wandering around, begging for money on the streets of Brazil. I was one of those children, and my parents were unbearable. At seven or eight years old, I remember seeing children with their mums and dads.

"I don't like the dad and mum you have given me," I told God. "Please give me new parents and a new family."

Around this same time, I went into the shopping centre and came across a group of people, L, her team, and A's family. I went over and asked them for some money.

"I don't have money," L replied. "But would you like something to eat?"

I said yes, and she told me about the children's project. That day, she took me to my mother.

My mother looked at me. "Do you want to go with her?"

"I do," I said immediately.

That was how the project became the family God gave to me.

I also remember when Auntie Shirley arrived at the project with some other missionaries. She didn't speak Portuguese, and we (the children) wanted to be able to communicate with her and the others in the team because they gave us so much love and care. God had answered this child's prayer for a family through this project.

Auntie Shirley was always there for us. She cooked for us, taught us to make cakes, took us out and made the effort to learn our language. When I was a teenager, she often took care of the house keys so we couldn't run away and get into trouble.

During my teenage years, I decided to leave the project, got involved with the wrong crowd and ended up pregnant. I asked the project director for help with my baby since my mum and family were all addicted to drugs, and I didn't want to abandon my daughter or leave her alone with them. I was on my own without her dad, living with different people. The director said I could stay in the project, but my child would eventually be put up for adoption. One day, the girls from the project went to Shirley's house, and somehow, Shirley invited me to live with her. Shirley never mentioned being separated from my daughter. She simply invited us to live with their family (her husband and daughter) with no conditions.

At that time, I was not working. Shirley supported and gave me advice, and with the mission's help, they renovated the house at the back so we could stay there. Shirley was counselling and guiding me. Those were such good times, but once again, because of my disobedience, I left, although Shirley was still there helping me despite my disobedience. Because of my wrong choices, I decided to follow the broad road, but Jesus had put her in my life so that I could continue on the narrow road. I chose wrongly and disobeyed.

A story that struck me during our devotional times was the prodigal son's story. Those times were the start of change and renewal, and I always compare myself with him - he had everything in his Father's house but chose to leave home and ended up eating the pig's food. However, when he remembered that even his father's servants ate at the table, he returned home. This scene really marked my life because now I didn't just have one child but two.

One day, years after leaving Shirley's house, I woke up feeling so emotional. There was nothing for the children to eat that day, not even bread or sugar. I went into the kitchen, sat down on a stool, and burst into tears. In my Father's house (with Shirley and her family), I had everything, but now I didn't even have Shirley's number. I wept desperately for my two children.

Suddenly, my phone pinged with a text message.

"Hi Ana, how are you?" It was Shirley. She still had my number!

"Auntie Shirley, I have nothing to eat," I replied. "I have nothing to give to my children. I am so desperate!"

Even when I deserved nothing and was so bad, God used Shirley's message to show me he cared about everything I was going through. Shirley immediately phoned and told me to come to her town for a food hamper.

I left the children at home and went to meet her, expecting a hamper. Instead, what she did meant everything. She took me food shopping. I kept loading the basics into the trolley, one packet of rice, a packet of beans.... Then she stopped me.

"The children need to eat well," she said. "Put in more milk, yoghurt, meat, chicken."

This might seem like a pinch of salt to some people, but it caused a change in my life as I realised that when we return to our Father's home, he gives us the best and much more. That day, God used Auntie Shirley to get me back on track. When I got home, I decided to return to the Cross, to Christ, and never drift away again. Today, three or four years later, despite difficult years full of troubles and battles, I continue on in God's ways.

Shirley kept communicating and staying in touch throughout the years. One of the last times we met was when we went to spend a day with her in Vila. Such pleasant moments as we shared what God had done in our lives.

"Ana, sometimes I keep thinking, so much work, but for what fruit?" She said, looking a bit troubled.

"Auntie Shirley, I am a fruit of your work," I replied. "Fruit you never turned your back on. When I needed it most as a child, you orientated me in the project and later took my baby and me in. And one more time, you looked for me and offered me food. Because of all your efforts, I am *now here in God's house with my family. I am fruit from the seed you planted in my heart when I was a child, a teenager, a young adult, and now a woman.*

What would have become of me, the baby and my two children without you? When you fed us that day, I took my first step towards Christ. No matter what comes my way, I am sure I will never leave the Lord again."

We kept in touch. One day, I approached her apprehensively, like a daughter talking to her mum.

'Mum, I'm pregnant again,' I said.

She gave me more advice that day and in other difficult times. She was concerned about my daughter's physical and spiritual well-being and that of my son. As well as helping me get back on track, Shirley invested in my daughter, a girl who didn't communicate or interact, by paying for her to go to camp. My daughter came back so different that my son also went to camp the following year. She continues to plant in our lives, and I believe she will plant in my grandchildren's lives, too.

I never had my mum or dad, but the Lord never abandoned me. He gave me Shirley to be a mother that I turn to when I need help, a friend and companion. Thank you from the bottom of my heart.

Aline – 25 years old

"I met the missionary Shirley (whom I affectionately call Auntie) in my teenage years. Upon arriving at the small Baptist congregation in my Vila, a long and beautiful story began that would impact my life and ministry. I grew up in church, always learning about God, but I made no commitment to him until a certain age, even though I was converted. After some time, Auntie Shirley drew me closer to God by demonstrating how good it is to serve the Lord.

When I was 13 or 14 years old, she gave me the opportunity to serve with her in a children's ministry called Clubinho. She kept giving me small tasks until I got to a very challenging one, which was telling Bible stories to the children. I allowed myself to be stretched with her help and developed in this area, the beginning of what the Lord was preparing for me.

After a while, she challenged me to lead that ministry, where I learned a lot and cultivated a love for the work I didn't even know was inside me. She continued to accompany me through counselling, youth meetings, and as my mentor.

Even though I was young, Auntie Shirley provided me with many missionary experiences, taking us to indigenous communities and villages, through which the Lord helped me understand my call. It wasn't easy, but she always supported and helped me (till today) with those decisions. Under Auntie Shirley's ministry, I had the greatest contact with mission opportunities to serve within the church, in camps, retreats, and on missionary trips, filling my heart with love for the work, God's Kingdom, and a desire to make Christ known to others. Her role in my life was extremely important and impactful.

Not long after completing high school, I went to study at the Word of Life Missionary Institute. God used Auntie Shirley to raise supporters and supplied everything I needed for my three-year course. While studying at Word of Life, God taught me, took care of my heart, and showed me that he had a greater purpose for me, which was the call to mission.

After Bible College, I returned to my church and started working there at the end of 2020. Today, I work with a project that seeks to reach youth with the gospel of Christ through sports at the Baptist Congregations in our Vila and in the town across the river. Today, I know the Lord wants to use me to reach others and make his name known through sport.

I believe the Lord led Auntie Shirley to our small community so that I and others could be reached. I am the result of Shirley Hough's missionary work. I give thanks to God for putting this incredible woman to walk alongside me since my teenage years."

—Aline, 25 years old,
now a missionary for the Baptist Congregation.

CHAPTER FOURTEEN
LIVING BY FAITH

"If you give them your *Uno* game, I will buy you another one when we get home!"

I was trying to persuade Thalia to give her game to the young Indian people. She had played *Uno* with them every day. It was a novelty, and they loved it.

"You can easily get another one, but they don't have the same access." I continued. "Trust me, Thalia, I will get you another one."

"Let me think about it," Thalia replied. She loved games, and *Uno* was her favourite. She had only just obtained her own. By the end of our time there, Thalia decided to sacrifice the game and left it with the tribe.

When we arrived home, I fulfilled my promise by buying her a new *Uno* game. Then, a few days later, a package addressed to Thalia arrived in the post. A friend from the UK had sent her a *Uno* game. WOW!

We were both taken aback, especially with the timing of it all. Thalia had sacrificed her one and only game of Uno and received back double. Only God could have done such a faith builder at the early stages of Thalia's faith. I was thrilled and touched by how God revealed himself to her so meaningfully in something insignificant that was important to Thalia. This is just one of many cases where God provided our every need, small or large.

He has never failed.

In this chapter, I will share how I learned to live by faith, with some amazing evidence of God providing for us even in the little details.

> *I have learnt that the better we know God, the more we will trust him, and the more we trust him, the more we will get to know him.* – Author unknown

During my early days in full-time ministry, I had never experienced living by faith and knew less about God in this respect. Looking back, I can testify that since leaving my job to follow God's call, I have never lacked anything. 25 years is a long time and a lot of living expenses, but these many years later, I know I can trust him. My faith may wobble from time to time, but God never fails.

Living by Faith

After my first visit to Brazil, various challenges lay ahead, one of which was to raise a support team. UFM gave me a target of raising £1,500.00 per month for my first four years in Brazil. This target seemed beyond me. How would I ever raise such an amount?!

Yet God is faithful. He provided for my every need and further stretched and strengthened my faith as I saw his provision.

By the summer of 2003, I was ready to head back to Brazil, meeting the deadline to fly out in September. But, a significant sum was missing from my financial target. UFM proposed that my planned September departure date should be postponed. This setback was extremely disappointing as I had nothing left to do in Durham. My degree and other activities were complete. What would I stay for?

At this point, God proved himself beyond anything I had ever experienced. Someone I hardly knew had heard about my predicament, and with one single donation, I had the £6,000.00 I needed and was free to go! I was stunned and overwhelmed! I'd never seen God's provision like this before. Tested until the last minute, but here I was, on schedule and ready to go on to the next chapter - my new life in Brazil!

Then, there was the day I was exhausted and stressed out from working on a college assignment with an approaching deadline. I had just been told we had to be at a social event for which I was to bake a cake. I couldn't even face the thought of making a cake, never mind taking the time to get the ingredients from the supermarket.

Testimonials

"Another 'finance event' that taught me to trust God more was during the time when we could not pay the workers. S began working for the project in 2000 when she was in her 50's. She is a quiet lady but so full of faith and such an encourager.

When we could not pay the workers on time, I went to their homes to explain the situation since they all had families to support and needed to know what was happening. One day, as I was handing out a small percentage of their money and apologising for the situation, S told me that I was the only one worrying about it. They knew I was speaking the truth to them and that they would receive what was owed as soon as possible and, in the meantime, God would provide for them all.

Apparently, she often got home from work to find a saucepan of beans or rice on her doorstep, left by a neighbour. She also did the same for her neighbours when she knew they were in dire financial straits."

M – Missionary colleague

Reluctantly, I got ready and headed out. Just then, a friend called out to me.

"Shirley, our church has just donated a food hamper to those of us who attend. Come over and see what you want."

I stepped into her kitchen to find several items laid out on the table.

"You go first," she said.

Right there was a bag of flour, just what I needed!

That day, I learned that God doesn't just care about the big things we need but also the smallest, like a bag of flour.

I didn't even need to go to the supermarket that day. I cried tears of joy as I realized how much my heavenly father cares for me!

We knew many Brazilians who had so little but never seemed to worry. They trusted God far more than we did and were contented living from hand to mouth. They might have no clue where the next meal was coming from, but they knew it would come. At the same time, when one person received something, they divided it out so that everyone had enough. Their customs and lessons in generosity were also key in touching, changing, and teaching me to think and act differently from the way I was brought up. I received pans of soup, fish, or *pupunha* (an Amazon palm tree fruit), meat, bottles of acai, bowls of fruit or *farinha* (flour made from cassava), cake, tapioca, and bags of Brazil nuts.

I understood that it was more blessed to give than to receive!

Then, there were mission trips and other ministry opportunities where the church would step out in faith, not knowing where the provision would come from, but willing and ready to go. They trusted that God would provide, and he always did. I was blessed and deeply challenged to see such faith. I also needed to think like this and display the same childlike faith. It gave a sense of freedom to seek God and obey what he wanted without being limited by financial costs.

Today, a congregation of ten or eleven adults (a few with fixed jobs) sustain the church and two girls in full-time ministry. They fund Bible college student placements and support a church plant. Their limited resources don't hamper them. Instead, they are generous and creative with what they have.

There have also been gifts and donations from the UK that enabled us to bless those around our ministry, buy land, do building work, support the project, and other endeavours.

On one occasion, a gift helped provide hundreds of Bibles in the Guajajara language so that nearly all the tribe's young people and many others had a Bible in their native language.

Isn't God good?! He has provided above and beyond what we have needed, not only sustaining us individually but blessing those to whom we ministered. It has been frequently humbling to be the bridge to bring financial blessings to our work and the lives we touch.

I, too, have been deeply blessed and encouraged.

CHAPTER FIFTEEN

GRACE GOES DEEPER STILL

"How much more can I take?" I cried out to God. "Is there no let up to the trials and battles? Will we ever know a "normal" in our lives together?"

We had been allowed "time out", but the separation was now greater, as we were thousands of miles apart on different sides of the world. Life had just been a full-on roller coaster of blessings and trials as we cared for those staying at Rescuing Hope and in the project, as well as the church. We were so ready for a break.

That day in December 2014, I was leaving for the UK. While waiting for my boarding call at the airport, we heard the awful news. Felipe had been denied a visa to travel to the UK. I was going two weeks ahead of him, and there was no time to do anything about it. I could only say goodbye and hope it would be sorted soon. I began my journey home.

Weeks of waiting, rescheduling his flight, and getting my hopes up followed, only to end in crushing disappointment. I cried out and asked God how much more I could take. Firstly, we had longed for this quality time together to rest, recuperate and process all we had been through. Now, we seemed to be in another battle – getting Felipe into the UK. It was a very emotional time with many questions.

As time went on, our communication became more strained, and I began to lose my peace. *Was there more to this? What was going on?* Something didn't feel right.

Despite all the stress, I was recuperating physically and emotionally. I started feeling stronger, having spent time and prayed with family and some dear friends. I was not only finding myself again, but I could start the New Year with fresh hope and direction. But where was my husband, and why wasn't God opening the way for him to join me?

Two months later, UFM and I researched and reviewed the visa requirements and put in a fresh application, confident it would be successful. At the same time, a niggling feeling began growing in me. Why was Felipe avoiding contact? Why so many unresolved issues when he had the time to sort things out? Was he in a mess with something he couldn't share with me? The stories I was hearing from Brazil did not match up.

I also asked UFM whether I should return to Brazil until the situation was sorted. But I was convinced this time in the UK was meant to be, and I'd only just arrived. Was it the right thing to do and the right stewardship of my finances? Deciding to seek God, I prayed he would reveal everything that was hidden. I had to fight for my marriage and ministry. We had already come through so many battles. Was something specific coming against us in the spiritual realm? Surely it was God's will for us to have this time out together?

While in prayer, I heard the phrase "flattering lips." I had no proof of what this meant, but my peace was gone. Others were also sensing the same – a piece of the jigsaw puzzle was missing. I just hadn't worked it out.

Finally, at the beginning of March, the disclosures began, many of them with huge implications. It was such a shock to my system and a struggle to believe. Over a week, I gained more information, and each day's revelation was more astounding than the last. I realize God's graciousness was allowing me to digest a little every day rather than hearing them at once. So much had been hidden from me, but God answered my prayer rather than let me be deceived any longer. He assured me that his favour was on me, and he was my Shield, so I could trust him to see me through.

Grace goes Deeper Still

I went through weeks of trauma, sensing evil at night, unable to sleep or eat properly. My family took turns to keep me company through the night. I had no idea how to cope with being lied to and deceived, but also with the aftermath. How was I to handle this? What direction was I to take? My feelings ranged from broken to hurt and betrayed. Everything I stood for had been violated. Yet another side of me still loved him. There was such a sense of loss.

I had said goodbye to Felipe at the airport, not realising I would never see him again. Had he known that when he let me go? Why had he carried on as normal?

Yet despite the brokenness, God's presence was tangible; his word was alive and constantly speaking, and I continuously listened to worship music to keep focused. God also brought my family close to me in such a precious way. I am ever grateful for all they did to carry me through this dark time.

Apart from them, I wanted to see no one. With no explanation, I was broken and confused, trying to understand what was going on with Felipe in Brazil and grappling with the issues before God. How could God have allowed them, and how did the matter glorify him? I had questions and no answers.

Made In Brazil

I also had no idea what attitude to take before Felipe because of what he was involved in. Part of me was so ashamed and wanted nothing to do with him. Also, what were the implications of contacting him?

I was so grieved.

A month later, I felt able to talk. It was a broken phone call on both sides. My heart cried for him, and I wished it were a bad dream! But there was clearly no return. He didn't open the possibility. He had turned his back on the Lord and wanted nothing more. I couldn't understand. What had driven him to all this?

As time went on, my heart was conflicted between aching for him and the need for justice. I longed for his restoration.

Identifying with the Cross

Easter arrived and impacted my life deeply as I realized afresh what it stood for because of my situation.

The Cross, a symbol of suffering, love, grace, and forgiveness, made me identify with Jesus' being betrayed, smashed and broken. Yet, he denied himself to offer us such love and forgiveness.

"Father, forgive them, for they know not what they do."
He cried from the cross.

Could I deny myself and my needs to offer such love and forgiveness? With this personal challenge, I was broken, in pain and sorrow.

♦♦♦♦♦♦♦♦

The only way back from sin is returning to Jesus through the Cross

Recognising that God offers a second chance and that his grace always goes deeper, I longed for Felipe to be brought afresh to the Cross.

I knew then that I needed TIME:

TIME to see how things would unfold

TIME to heal

TIME before I could consider going to Brazil

TIME before I could decide on the future

And so, life carried on here in the UK, mostly with my family. But, despite their company and fun, I felt alone, with no close friends and no life here. My life was in Brazil, and there were so many questions about what the future held.

As Matt Redman's song says, God's grace goes deeper than our shame, and when we cannot heal our own soul, he alone can do what is necessary.

Everything had been unexpectedly stolen from me. My dreams were shattered, and I was torn between two lives, two countries, and two cultures. Disheartened and discouraged, I would slip into thinking negatively, and the only thing to do was to refocus by pushing into God by listening to praise music.

In April, a friend sent me a card saying she believed I would return to Brazil and that God would do more than I had ever dreamed. I would also see many coming out of bondage. This word stirred a glimmer of hope within me.

Was this not the end? Would I return to Brazil?

A line from a hymn became my prayer: *"Sanctify to me thy deepest distress."*

I was here for time out and restoration, but now faced an intensified battle with deeper and more complicated problems. I asked God to continue to mould and make me through this awful experience.

The desire to return to Brazil gradually stirred up within me, and then a friend from the Pavement project came to visit. It was God's special touch when I needed it most! I thought I'd lost it all, but my heart pulled towards Brazil again.

Over the months, I grew stronger and less broken despite more disappointing information coming to light from Brazil.

In July, a close friend came to stay, and we had some wonderful spiritual fellowship that spurred me on and brought fresh motivation, hope and faith. She gave me a prophetic word that provided hope and a sense of direction from God.

"Now may the God of hope fill you with all joy and peace in believing, that you may ABOUND in hope by the power of the Holy Spirit." Romans 15:13

Surely, this was what God wanted: to give me HOPE. Wasn't Rescuing HOPE the ministry we had been doing?

"...I will rebuild its ruins and I will set it up...says the Lord who does all these things" Acts 15: 16-17

When God called me to Brazil, he used Isaiah 58:11 to speak so much to me about being used in restoring and rebuilding. It was my turn to hold on to hope and fight the battle for restoration in prayer. If we believed it for our ministry to others, I had to believe that it was God's will to rebuild and restore my situation.

My friend emphasised LOVE would help with the restoration. If I truly loved Felipe, I would wait. WAIT, another word God kept bringing to my attention.

"My soul, wait silently for God alone, for my expectation is from him. He only is my rock and my salvation, he is my defense, I shall not be moved."
Psalm 62:5-6

To LOVE would be costly and meant going against the flow. Many might not understand or agree, but love required self-denial in not dwelling on my hurts and what Felipe had done to me. Costly love would trust God to protect me.

To WAIT was so important as it was still too early. I needed to "let go and let God", not rush the work of restoration, but let God bring it full circle in HIS time. The perfect picture I saw was of a caterpillar cocooning itself to become a butterfly. If the cocoon opens too soon, the butterfly and the beauty for which it is designed will be lost. This was a powerful picture and an instruction not to rush or interfere with the beautiful tapestry God wanted to weave with my life.

Months later, I heard a sermon where the preacher said, "...*Whoever loves deeply can forgive*". I *had* forgiven Felipe and was now concerned about his (mostly spiritual) well-being and restoration. However, I had much to express to him but still couldn't.

God gave me many dreams, and there were times when I sensed evil or felt the need to pray and intercede for Felipe. In these moments, God focused me on himself and reminded me through certain worship songs that he is a warrior who fights for us, that he is the Lord of Hosts, the God of angel armies, and the great Lion of Judah who, with his almighty power can scatter our enemies and dispel evil, darkness and oppression. Felipe had been taken captive by the enemy, but God could ably deliver and set him free.

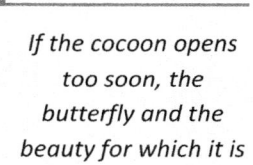

If the cocoon opens too soon, the butterfly and the beauty for which it is designed will be lost.

As time went on, I let go, focused and got involved with friends, family, church and even a camp, finding healing and becoming myself again. With peace and freedom returning, I relaxed and started enjoying life once more.

I was ready to return to Brazil, to sort out practical things like the house, and finally meet with Felipe face to face.

CHAPTER SIXTEEN

TESTED BY FIRE

As I prepared to return and confront the situation in Brazil, there were fears in my heart.

What would I find?
How would people receive me?
How would I cope or handle everything?

I had many questions and mixed emotions and knew people would also be watching my reactions, so I prayed for my life to be a testimony and glorify God in all things.

God was speaking and preparing my heart

Despite all Felipe had done, there was love for him, and I continually prayed that God would give him eyes to see, ears to hear, a mind to understand and a heart to respond. I prayed for a miracle, healing, and complete restoration, as well as a renewed, powerful, and effective ministry that would give others hope through his testimony.

A close friend had said, "Shirley, God has entrusted you with this challenge -- to pray for Felipe's restoration!"

This challenge needed patient hope and the certainty that God would act to bring about his good purposes. I had many personal struggles and questions, yet God continually reminded me of the glorious future awaiting us with him, of his care, and my security in him despite my insecure circumstances.

I remember being at some cliffs overlooking the Irish Sea on one such occasion. The waves were crashing about the rocks below, yet a few birds perched in the cleft of the rock. Because the rock was solid, the birds were secure, just like my life was secure on the rock that is Christ despite the storm and waves around me.

> *"So, while I bear the cross and meet the storms and billows wild, Jesus, for my soul is caring, 'naught can harm his father's child[21]."*

This theme of being entrusted reoccurred on various occasions. One was a quote from Helen Roseveare in my devotional:

---

[21] He Will Hide Me – Hymn by Mary E Servoss (Public Domain)

"He could have prevented what was happening to her but had chosen for his own sovereign purpose to allow her to pass through the experience, even if she never knew why. It came to the point that, even though abused and wickedly so, she responded,

'...OK, Lord, I thank you for trusting me with this, even though I don't understand.'

In accepting the Lord was in control and that what she was experiencing was in some mysterious way for his glory, the situation was transformed, and she knew remarkable peace."

"God would have me hold to my appointed furrow even though my plough be wet with tears[iv]."

And another quote from Helen Roseveare:

"God will engineer our circumstances and daily lives so that he can thereby make us like Jesus. This takes the sting out of much that would otherwise hurt us. He allows happenings and accidents to occur, things which will affect us deeply, perhaps, only so that, through them, we may be drawn closer to himself."

I was discovering this to be so true. I had been and was being drawn closer to him through the situation. I wanted to rise to the challenge God had entrusted to me and not feel sorry for myself anymore. I wanted to fight and be available to all God wanted to accomplish. He entrusted the challenge to me, and my prayer was that I would respond in a way which glorified him.

It was my turn to wait. Felipe had waited for me all those years before, and I was now determined to wait for him, responding with love instead of vengeance so as to impact him. I knew this love was not from me and prayed God would give me an appointment to see him.

There was one more thing to deal with.

Just before I was to travel, a couple in church lost a baby, and the reality of my two losses finally hit me, especially the second baby for whom I had never grieved. It seemed more heightened and painful because there might no longer be a further chance of a pregnancy. It was a harrowing few days.

I had kept myself pure before marriage and been faithful in this area. I also had a heart for children and a desire for my own, so why would God allow this? Why did other people prosper in their sin while I honoured God and seemed to lose out? I was having to come to terms with possibly never having my own children, yet I had to keep trusting God. Otherwise, how would I continue? Questioning it too deeply could knock my own faith.

A real fear kicked in as though I was being robbed of my peace about going to Brazil, with thoughts including, *Would I be in danger? Would I cope?* Again, I refocused by getting my eyes back on the Lord and regained my peace through reading Psalm 91 and Exodus 33.

I also read a quote where someone complained to God that a job was too great, and God replied, "For one, yes, but not for two. Have faith! Have I not said that I WILL see you through?"

On the 6th of September 2015, I arrived back in Brazil, full of peace.

It was like coming Home!

Immediately, though, further news came about what Felipe had done that threatened to overcome me with grief, anger, embarrassment and concern about my reputation and testimony as his wife. Yet God gently reassured me that he was with me. I even received a very pertinent text en route, and the person who sent it had no idea of my return.

7 things God wants you to know today:
- *Don't be afraid.*
- *I love you.*
- *Trust in me.*
- *I will help you.*

- *Don't be discouraged.*
- *Follow me.*
- *I AM with you.*

I arrived in Belem steeped in pain and sadness and yet feeling cocooned and protected. It was a new chapter that felt so right. The church family warmly received me again, giving me peace and reassurance as they reconfirmed and recognised my call and place amongst them. I felt at home and wanted to be usable and available once again.

Another devotional reading spoke so clearly to me one day:

> *"Vengeance may break a man's spirit.*
> *Kindness will break his heart."*
> *What wants to retaliate in me, be restrained.*
> *Be crucified – "Not I, but Christ.*
> *That to thy honor, I be not easily provoked.*
> *That when reviled, I revile not you*[22]*."*

The three months back in Brazil were bittersweet – mainly harrowing but with moments of joy. God's presence was real, and as Nehemiah 8:10 says, the joy of the Lord was my strength. God spoke continually, right to each emotion I

---
[22] Source unknown.

went through. My close relationships within the church and with the missionaries were precious. Then there was Adriana, the amazing friend who walked with me as someone to talk things through step by step, enabling me to process, reflect and respond. Only God could have done this so perfectly. I felt carried and strengthened to go forward with people by my side each step of the way.

Another devotional based on Psalm 94:19 read,

"In the multitude of my anxieties within me, thy comforts delight my soul."

> "Tranquility of soul, in the midst of turmoil, an enveloping peace while the storm still rages... Although the disturbing thoughts are still within, they are transmuted by divine comforts...The trials his infinite wisdom does not remove, his inexhaustible love will share, and his invincible power will control... Through the Word, the Holy Spirit can transmute pain into comfort and crushing sorrow into sweetness."[23]

This was so true.

I had also grappled with whether I would ever return to ministry in Brazil, but a precious moment occurred soon

---

[23] Source unknown.

after my arrival. While listening to a sermon in church, my eyes fell on Genesis 28:15,

> "Behold, I am with you and will keep you wherever you go and will bring you back to this land, for I will not leave you until I have done what I have spoken to you".

It was as though God whispered, *Shirley, you will be coming back. There is more!*

> "Out of deepest pain has come strongest conviction of the presence of God and of the love of God."
> Paul Mallard — Invest in your Suffering

The enemy seeks to destroy, but the victory is ours. God gave me this challenge, knowing he could trust me with it. This renewed sense of calling spurred me on to continue to fight and pray.

As time went on, I was happier and more content as I started moving on emotionally and getting used to being on my own again. There was much to sort out at the house, but we seemed to resolve matters effortlessly. God appeared to be protecting our comings and goings, especially now I had no car and had to rely on public transport and its added risks.

One day, while thinking about the cross I had to bear, I reflected on what it meant to share in Christ's sufferings. He, too, was shamed, yet he loved and forgave. I did feel overwhelmed at times with how much I had to deal with and what a future alone might look like, questioning whether to get a divorce. I desired Felipe's repentance and restoration, and in other moments, I wanted nothing to do with him. Anguished choices that I felt incapable of making. Sometimes, the desire for companionship was so real and I felt vulnerable and incapable of going on. Again, God reassured me:

> *"When my heart is overwhelmed, lead me to the rock that is higher than I."* Psalm 61:2

The questions were endless.

- ❖ *Why had God allowed all this?* Surely, a broken Christian marriage of two missionaries (one a pastor) doesn't glorify him.
- ❖ *Did I get my guidance wrong?* Surely not, or how could I be where I am in this church today?
- ❖ *Should I move on with life?* Didn't I need to see Felipe first? Simply moving on felt so wrong.

Yet God's ways are PERFECT – Psalm 18:30

God knows us. Even on the darkest night, we must remind ourselves that he is making plans for us.

I need to trust that his way is PERFECT.

God is all-seeing and all-knowing

What we cannot understand in the government of the nations or in our own lives, God asks us to accept – knowing that he is truly good and does good. His all-wise, all-seeing plans are devised with attentive loving-kindness.

He drew my attention to two consistent themes in Brazil. To continually pray and intercede for Felipe, break the enemy's plans on my knees and believe God for his life. He might be sinking in the mud and mire, but God could draw him out, place his feet on a rock, and put a new song in his mouth[24]. I was to use my God-given gifts and talents, fight, and persevere. The greater the victory, the greater the fight to attain it, but we must fight. My mission wasn't complete and would involve dying to self, forgiving, and not seeking revenge despite any shame or injustices.

> "The enemy is often allowed to inflict his wounds so that godly saints can shine even more brightly in the crucible."

---

[24] Psalm 40:2-3

The other theme was suffering. I was understanding something about fire and how God works in it.

> *"That the genuineness of your faith, being much more precious than gold that perishes, though it is tested by fire, may be found to praise, honor and glory at the revelation of Jesus Christ."* 1 Peter 1:7

As gold is heated to remove the impurities, so God uses times when our lives are 'heated up' to make us more like him. The hotter the fire, the more beautiful the gold.

> *"...For I consider that the sufferings of this present time are not worthy to be compared with the glory which shall be revealed in us .... For we know that all things work together for good to those who love God, to those who are called according to his purpose, for whom he foreknew, he also predestined to be conformed to the image of his Son, that he might be the firstborn among many brethren."* - Romans 8:18, 28-29

What is God's purpose in our sufferings according to these verses?

- That he might reveal his glory IN us
- That we might be conformed to the image of his Son.

Suffering doesn't distance us from God, but it helps us identify with Jesus.

Tested By Fire

"In times of adversity, our roots are forced down to hidden rivers, driven to prayer, to seek the warmth of God's presence... and spiritual growth prospers[25]."

The more a precious stone is polished, the more it reflects the image of the person looking at it. Trials and suffering put pressure on us, and if we seek God, he can use them to transform us into his likeness through our attitudes to the problem, how we react, and what we do and say. People watching us will be impacted by how we face these difficulties.

- Do we trust Christ despite unanswered questions?
- Can we love when it is hard?
- Can we continue being shining lights in a perverse and corrupt generation?

The sufferings of this present time don't even compare to the glory being revealed within us (Christ in us is the Hope of glory) as we become more like him each day.

James tells us to count it as joy when we go through the trials, knowing they form character in us[26], and God is preparing those who don't give up to receive our crown of life.

---

[25] Author unknown
[26] James 1:2, 3

Our focus is eternity

My thoughts were very much on this - all these things are preparing us for something far greater. And our focus needs to be on that. Trials can weigh us down and make us sad, but we have a surpassing glorious hope - **Jesus is coming back one day.** So many times, his word tells us, "I am coming!"

> *"Behold the Lord God shall come... Behold his reward is with him..."* Isaiah 40:10

Focusing on these truths gives us renewed hope and joy despite our current circumstances, sufferings and difficulties. We are to be faithful until the end to receive the crown of Life.

Today, I am in God's school, learning great truths and learning how to apply them to my life. It is not always easy, but it is definitely best to understand what it means to:

- ❖ Love as Jesus did.
- ❖ Repay evil with good and recognise that
- ❖ Love covers a multitude of sins.

"Love bears all things, believes all things, hopes all things, endures all things, Love NEVER fails."
– 1 Corinthians 13:7

The gospel brings hope to those in the deepest pits of sin. NOTHING is impossible with God; he can transform any life.

I discovered and am still learning that waiting is the hardest thing. I couldn't establish any contact with Felipe. Apparently, he disappeared just before I arrived in Brazil. Having tried various links and contacts, I found that proved to be true, which is an even greater test of faith. Still without answers or explanations, I follow in obedience to God's word and trust God for him.

God's ways are PERFECT. With precision, he will keep his schedule, which is usually hidden from us, to test our faith.

> *"Now faith is the substance of things hoped for, the evidence of things not seen."* Hebrews 11:1

Hosea, the prophet, was another person through whom God taught me. He obeyed God's instruction to marry a prostitute, love her unconditionally, and continually take her back no matter what she did. It's a love that bears all things and never fails.

A friend suggested that I should not divorce Felipe but wait to see what God was going to do. This was the test in the furnace of countless pressures to disown and divorce him. But she explained that my choices now would determine the future. The enemy was tempting me to give up on my faith for his restoration, to conform, and by so doing, grant the enemy the leeway to destroy both Felipe and God's purpose.

This took blind faith! I hadn't a clue where Felipe was, who he was involved with, what he was doing. I simply had to hold on and trust that God is enough. He is far greater, much higher; he is my defence, my protector and my lawyer.

God has everything mapped out and knows how much to trust us with. It is a process in which he entrusts a little more to us each time he sees that we are ready. No one can find out the work God does from beginning to end.

> *"Can you search out the deep things of God? Can you find out the limits of the Almighty?"* – Job 11:7

> *"He has made everything beautiful in its time."*
> – Ecclesiastes 3:11

Another turning point

As I reflected on all God was teaching me through his Word and through friends, I reached a turning point, and by October, a cloud lifted, and I began to see my way forward. With fresh conviction, I knew I had to make the right choices and take my stand. Several doors opened that would have been so comfortable to enter, but God's still, small voice kept tugging at my heart with concern for the unreached who had never heard the gospel.

A friend and I visited a young girl from our church at the New Tribes Mission, where I got a feel for the mission, its work and training. The pull was so strong that I enquired about their course, Shekinah, believing this was the next step.

To my disappointment, they would not consider me because I was separated. And there it was – another obstacle on my journey into Christian ministry - the stigma of the separated Christian. Another "why?" with no explanation. This is not what I would have desired, but it happened, and I now find myself in this predicament.

A Brazilian song, *Tenho um Chamado* (*I Have a Call*), lay so deeply on my heart in those final weeks in Brazil, once again bringing a firm conviction to my heart. I couldn't stop. I must continue. Despite all coming against me, the great I AM had called and sent me, and there was no time to look back with so much to do.

God's call was still on my life. How could I remain quiet when thousands have never heard the gospel. No matter how much the enemy worked to take me out of ministry, I would keep fighting.

Made In Brazil

Not long after, I was thrilled to hear that New Tribes Mission would reconsider my case to study with them. I had heard God right! It took another couple of months before I received the final decision, and oh, what joy, I was accepted! God is faithful, and his plans cannot be thwarted. He chose me and was sending me out.

"This is the way, walk in it..." Isaiah 30:21 was one of my readings shortly after receiving the news. Then, I received another beautiful confirmation during my last days in Brazil. Leaving Belem had been hard, and I was quite emotional. I was returning to the other side of the world where any hope of hearing from or contacting Felipe would be practically impossible. I spent my last few days in Rio de Janeiro, where I visited my friend's church. She wanted to introduce me to a dear 102-year-old friend who was once a pastor.

The man took my hand in his frail one and gave me a precious, anointed word from God. He spoke of the vast mission field in Brazil and quoted Isaiah 6:8, the verse God used to call me to Brazil when I was still in Faith Mission Bible College.

"How shall they hear unless someone is sent?" He continued.

Those words from Romans 10:14 felt like a precious recommissioning just as I was leaving Brazil. He also confirmed that I would return.

"Behold, I am with you and will keep you wherever you go, and will bring you back to this land; for I will not leave you until I have done what I have spoken to you." Genesis 28:15

CHAPTER SEVENTEEN

COVENANT LOVE

2016 began with the sense of a fresh start despite the uncertainties, especially considering Proverbs 3:5:

> *"TRUST in the Lord with ALL your heart and lean NOT on your own understanding."*

I had come through a full cycle in 2015 and was back where I started. It was time to move on with focus. God's call had remained clear throughout my recent trials.

> *"And so I have made it my aim to preach the gospel, not where Christ was named, lest I should build on another man's foundation."* Romans 15:20

This world is still in a mess and needs a Saviour. The good news must be shared with those who haven't heard it.

My passion and desire was to be available to the Lord.

His love so amazing, so divine, demands my soul, my life, my ALL!

And I wanted to give him my ALL.

ALL I am and have and will be, ALL for him.

There was no turning back from all God had for me.

I don't understand all that has happened, and there is more to come, but my life is in his hands, and I can trust him.

God had set an open door before me that no man could shut, and this was confirmed when my pastor and the UFM leadership both expressed their full support for me to continue. Then, a few weeks later, the opportunity came to be equipped and trained at New Tribes Mission to take the gospel to unreached people groups.

Behold, I do a NEW thing

I also wrestle to understand Rescuing Hope. Surely, there was more to this vision, yet that is also currently in his hands. I believe it will be fulfilled in time and within a family context. Many children in Brazil are in desperate need, and my heart cries for them, but I must be where God wants me, which, at this point, is heading down a new and different path.

God knew I needed time to fully recuperate, heal and be restrengthened. The Rescuing Hope type of ministry is a real battle to set children free, and I believe God will use this change of direction to strengthen and restore me. Only he knows what lies ahead.

I started the new year with renewed HOPE and trust and confidence in my good Shepherd, who has led me and kept me so far and will continue to do so.

> *"Behold I do a NEW thing."* (Isaiah 43:19)

The words of the song *I'm Waiting* from the movie *Fireproof* summed it up perfectly as I set out into 2016. I would move ahead boldly and confidently, continuing to serve him while waiting despite all the challenges.

As the year progressed, God continued to heal my heart, enabling me to focus on other things. The times spent with my family were precious and God-ordained as he worked out his plans and purposes there, too. I resumed my "Home Assignment" and visited my supporting churches, fellowships and friends who were praying for me, all of which were an immense joy and source of encouragement.

I have realized the benefits and long-lasting effects of having the time out both as a person and for future ministry. However, God kept confirming his word and promises, asking me to WAIT.

> *"I WAIT for the Lord ... and in HIS Word do I hope."*
> Psalm 130:5 (KJV)

"God is not a man that he should lie... Has He said, and will He not do?
Or has He spoken, and will He not make it good?"
Numbers 23:19 (NKJV)

"Blessed is [she] who believes, for there WILL be a fulfilment of those things which were told her from the Lord."
Luke 1:45

"To move man, through God, by prayer alone."

"Shall not the Judge of all the earth do right?"
Gen 18:25

"As for God, His ways are PERFECT." Psalm 18:30

"TRUST in the Lord with ALL your heart and lean not on your own understanding." Proverbs 3:5

Being able to have *one* conversation with Felipe for closure and understanding proved impossible. I learned firsthand how difficult it was to wait, unable to do anything other than believe in the power of prayer and put that into practice. It was completely out of my hands.

The life of Joseph taught me that God was bringing me into position and that what was meant for evil, he was working for good. Over the year, I also learned about covenant love and came to understand, through John Piper's teachings, the true meaning of a God-ordained marriage as

God's picture of his covenant love to his church. The church often fails in our relationship with God, but he never fails us. We are also to display the gospel, which is God's covenant of unconditional love, mercy, and grace. This love will not let us go!

God revealed that the covenant in the marriage vows I took before him was for better or worse. This was 'the worse' and despite it appearing to be over, with Felipe giving no place for reconciliation, I was responsible for my vow to love him, for better or worse, unconditionally as a testament to God's covenant love and grace towards us.

One day, I sat looking at my wedding ring, and the children's chorus we sang in Sunday School suddenly took on a profound meaning:

> *"God's love is like a circle, a circle big and round.*
> *And you know that to a circle, no ending can be found.*
> *And so, the Love of Jesus goes on eternally,*
> *Forever and forever, I know that God loves me!"*

I visualized God's grace, mercy and love in a way I had never comprehended until my heart softened and changed.

Love NEVER fails

Love is a powerful spiritual weapon. I had to deny myself and my feelings, take up my cross and follow Christ's example. To die to self like that grain of wheat and bring forth life and more fruit.

I was to love Felipe back to God from the pit and show him the mercy and grace the Father demonstrated in the parable of the prodigal son from the supernatural work God was doing in my heart. He was transforming me through the renewing of my mind and thought patterns, and I was being conformed to Christ's image. As Romans 8:28, 29 puts it, God was working it all together for good to make me more like him. Profound, amazing!

To show this practically, I put my wedding ring back on as a testimony of covenant love. Felipe never witnessed this, but God was working in me, and as I obeyed, he continued moving me into the position where his purposes and plans could be outworked.

These were challenging days, with nothing externally encouraging me that something was happening. In fact, restoration felt more and more impossible because of the distance and lack of contact between me and Felipe.

But my conviction that God was at work grew. God wasn't finished yet; this was only the beginning of a "Glorious Unfolding", as Steve Curtis Chapman's song describes.

A breakthrough would come.

CHAPTER EIGHTEEN

SERVE YOU WHILE I AM WAITING

"It totally frustrates the devil that he can do nothing to get you out of God's plan for your life. He attacks your body, but you become stronger. He causes you to suffer losses, yet your love for God grows deeper. His attacks on your family and relationships only make you seek God more. That resilience is the quality of a soldier. God's choosing you as his soldier doesn't numb you to pain or mean you always feel brave, that you never face disheartening, burdensome challenges, and never fall or make mistakes. Whatever happens, you simply commit to moving forward in God, and no matter the obstacle, you find a way to come out on top. You are a champion and an unstoppable soldier of Christ[27]."

---

[27] Source Unknown

> *"Brethren, I do not count myself to have apprehended; but one thing I do, forgetting those things which are behind and reaching forward to those things which are ahead, I press toward the goal for the prize of the upward call of God in Christ Jesus."*
> – Philippians 3:13-14

Facing the future

With no answers or solutions, I decided to move forward, focusing on what God had been speaking into my heart. I couldn't dwell on the past, but I could continue to fulfil God's call on my life, knowing much more was unfolding. I believe God was preparing me for new spheres of service and crossing paths once again with people who would become such precious friends.

I returned to Goías, Brazil, for a fresh start through practical training on the New Tribes Mission's Shekinah course. What a change to life.

The course covered a variety of topics, and we were soon busy with linguistic subjects, including grammar in different languages, phonetics, translation, anthropology, health, literacy, church planting, and Christian character. The practical lessons included electric installations and soldering.

Our afternoons involved practical work and college maintenance, which taught us new skills like painting, decorating, cleaning, maintaining the guest house and hospitality. I also learned to play volleyball, with weekly competitive games.

For one month, we took ACL (Acquisition of Language and Culture), practical lessons in which the staff did simulations. We imagined we were spending time with a tribe of indigenous people and had to observe and learn their culture, vocabulary, and grammatical patterns. This inspired our learning and gave us greater insight and experience. After this, we did a month-long placement in an indigenous tribe, where we put the ACL lessons into practice.

We also had a survival camp in the wild. Two single girls, a married couple, and I set up our tents a short distance from the other teams for a month, with challenges to develop our base and build a toilet, shower, and kitchen with a brick/mud oven. The skills and knowledge we acquired through this experience were amazing. I was surprised at our achievements. Other training included sailing two kinds of boats on a lake and a small river with the challenges involved. We learned to ration and preserve our food and to use the surrounding natural resources. A small brook nearby was our water supply for that month.

What did I gain from all this? We can live with very little and be content. With no internet or outside communication, the time allowed us to value and build good relationships with one another.

The course was refreshing and just what I needed. So much that I learned will be useful for observing and learning from unknown cultures and languages.

I made more friends as God further expanded my boundaries in Brazil, with a tremendous knowledge of the indigenous people groups, their needs and the challenges of the gospel and missionary work.

> *"And so, I have made it my aim to preach the gospel, not where Christ was named, lest I should build on another man's foundation...."* - Romans 15:20

Zealous to reach them, the above verse stayed with me, along with the reassurance that God's call was still on my life. I must follow after the call and announce the gospel wherever God would send me.

During this time, I got involved with a ministry at the female prison near the college. It was a joy to sit in the cells weekly, listen to the women's stories and share God's word with them.

Made In Brazil

I will never forget Graduation Day in June 2018. To have completed the course in my second language, started afresh in Brazil, be recommissioned for God's service, along with the new friendships and training I received, overwhelmed me emotionally. Deeply grateful to God on that special day, I wondered what lay ahead. I couldn't go into the work of New Tribes Mission because of my marriage situation, but I knew God opened this door for a reason that hadn't been revealed to me yet.

Entrusted

During my time at NTM, another turn of events changed my life again. Thalia, who stayed with us when she was two, now lived with her sister a few hours from NTM. However, their circumstances changed, and social services approached me to see if I could offer Thalia a home.

I didn't want to turn my back on her, but how would this all fit together with my studies? I prayed and sought advice from my mission leadership and close friends. What was God saying and outworking? Surely, my geographical closeness to Thalia was no mistake. God makes no mistakes!!

As I considered the situation in prayer, during devotions and at various times of the day, the Word "entrusted" came to me in the sentence:

This is one of the ones I have entrusted to your care.

Then, various Scriptures and thoughts came to my attention to back up what I had heard along the following lines:

"Fear not, for I am with you; Be not dismayed, for I am your God. I will strengthen you, yes, I will help you, I will uphold you with My righteous right hand." Isaiah 41:10

"You have what it takes to bring home my precious ones – you have me! When you walk with me, you shine!"

God gives us HIS resources to carry the trouble appointed for each day. What are you AND the Holy Spirit going to do today? For us who know Him, we are not on our own. It's us AND him together!

"Sometimes you just have to go for it and see what happens!"

One day, while reading, the following words crystallised it for me:

> *"To trust God is to know that,*
> *Our way God designs.*
> *Our story God writes.*
> *The time God determines.*
> *And the victory he decrees[28]!"*

---

[28] Source unknown

Made In Brazil

So, I agreed to be considered as her guardian, entrusting to God and his timing to open or shut the door according to his will for us. And he had it all worked out. At the end of the guardianship evaluation process, a year later, I had completed my course and could bring Thalia to live with me, give her my full attention and focus on caring for her needs.

God was also starting to show me that Rescuing Hope wasn't over. The dream wasn't shattered by the events that happened. He merely had a different plan to complete what he laid on my heart. I was learning again that His ways and plans are not ours. He made me understand that while I didn't have natural children, he was fulfilling his promises through my legally adopting Thalia and through many other children who considered me their mum.

> *"'Sing, O barren, You who have not borne!*
> *Break forth into singing and cry aloud,*
> *You who have not laboured with child!*
>
> *For more are the children of the desolate than the children of the married woman," says the Lord.*
> *"Enlarge the place of your tent, and let them stretch out the curtains of your dwellings;*
> *Do not spare;*
> *Lengthen your cords and strengthen your stakes.*
> *For you shall expand to the right and to the left...."*

*Do not fear, for you will not be ashamed;
Neither be disgraced, for you will not be put to shame;
For you will forget the shame of your youth,
And will not remember the reproach of your widowhood anymore.*

*For your Maker is your husband,
The Lord of hosts is His name;
And your Redeemer is the Holy One of Israel;
He is called the God of the whole earth*

*For the Lord has called you
Like a woman forsaken and grieved in spirit."' -
Isaiah 54:1-6 (NKJV)*

The process unfolded effortlessly. God's hand was so evident in the open door, and her adoption was granted the following year! God's ways are PERFECT.

We returned to live at the Vila after graduation while waiting to complete these processes, adjusting to life together. God opened further ministry doors and opportunities to teach English to a children's group at church and to give individual lessons to teenage girls from the village. I also started discipling a few newly married couples in the church. Opportunities for prayer and counselling, as well as mobilizing the church to mission, came up, enhancing the freedom, joy, and simplicity within the Vila's rural setting. These and caring for Thalia became means of healing for me.

Life moved on. For legal reasons, a divorce had to be filed, and as we were caught up in all God was doing in and through us in this new chapter, we left the past behind.

The church had kept in touch with the Guajajara Indians and the work there, and it now felt right to organize another visit, this time offering the opportunity to anyone from the church rather than choosing individuals. This allowed God to select and lead the team, which ended up being fourteen of us. It thrilled my heart to see him at work during the preparation time and on the trip itself. Most of them didn't have the financial resources but stepped out in faith, trusting God to provide what they needed.

Once again, their simple faith blessed, challenged and taught me so much. How many times do we set a budget and check for all the resources before we can go?

As always, God didn't fail them. It was the first mission trip for many of the team, as well as being so far from home. The team comprised of married and single adults, young people, teenagers, children, and even whole families. By dividing ourselves up to work with each age group within the tribe, we achieved far more as strong friendships were

Serve You While I Am Waiting

formed, the gospel was shared, and fellowship and new adventures were enjoyed together.

We reported back at the church service on our return, and it was a joy to listen to each testimony of what God did through the experience. There was barely a dry eye in the building that night; everyone was deeply moved, blessed, and inspired to do more for God. I have included some comments and testimonies here for you to read.

> *"I never imagined myself leaving the Vila on a trip like this! I was used to going to the next town and back. I laid the costs of travel and the other necessities before the Lord in prayer and set aside a little at a time. To my surprise, I managed to get the whole amount to pay my way!*
>
> *When we arrived, what touched me was the people's willingness to sit and listen to God's Word without owning Bibles. They never grumbled or complained about the time, and their punctuality left a mark on me. They were always there when the pastor marked the register, with many coming early, ready and eager to hear the Word. There was no set finishing time, but they stayed until the service naturally finished. They were keen to memorise God's word, taking notes of the memory verse for each day. The way they received and looked after us really touched me, too." - C*

Made In Brazil

> *"What impacted me during this visit to Maranhão was that in a place so far away from everything else, God's Word reached communities that were difficult to access so that they could hear the gospel. God works in ways we can never imagine and knows all things and all possibilities." – P*

My own highlight was five-year-old Kalebe, the youngest team member. While making bracelets with beads, the colours of the wordless book with him and Thalia, I explained what each colour represented when presenting the gospel to someone and challenged them to share the gospel using the bracelet. I never dreamed that, during one of the next children's meetings, Kalebe would clearly tell the story of the wordless book to the whole group.

He went on to amaze us further during one of the youth meetings, saying he felt the urge to share the message with them, too. When we gave him a slot, the youth were gripped to see the tiny boy bringing the message articulately. God used him immensely in those meetings. No one is too old or young to be used by God; our willingness is what matters. Place your life in God's hand, and he will take, fill, and use what you have.

As previously mentioned, one of the girls had returned to work full-time with the tribe, and the trips were a stepping-stone to her discovering God's heart and will for her life. It was a joy to be part of it.

We just never know where a step of obedience will lead and the doors it can open for others.

The same year, we did another mission trip to a tiny, isolated community two hours across the river from us. We offered the opportunity to the entire church, and most of them stepped up to participate, so we divided up the teams as before.

We were in the house where we were staying, getting ready for the final evangelistic meeting, when Kalebe came up to his parents and me, looking seriously burdened.

'I have spoken to the children and youth,' he said. 'Can I have a slot to share with the adults?'

Since we recognized his God-given burdens and that the Lord had used him mightily on the previous trip, we readily gave him this opportunity.

To see this anointed five-year-old boy, so zealous and so used of God, is one aspect of mission work that I can only treasure in my heart. These were moments I never imagined or asked for, where God just stepped in and moved.

Kalebe walked through the grassy trail with me to the meeting, his Bible tucked under his arm.

Made In Brazil

'Auntie, I need to be your shadow,' he piped up. 'I want to learn everything I can from you, like a little missionary, so that I can grow up to do the same!'

The villagers sat in the chairs arranged in rows outside the house we were using. As the meeting went on, sure enough, Kalebe was given his little moment to participate and share with the adults. He got up with his Bible and children's visual story cards and solemnly and clearly shared the gospel with all who had gathered. Many marvelled to see such a little boy speaking so clearly, with such conviction and passion, sharing the good news of Jesus.

Only God knows where this little life will end up, but Kalebe continues to be a faithful evangelist and testimony to the Lord wherever he goes. He is also a real partner in the gospel and in prayer. Kalebe has frequently inspired and spurred me on, rebuking and challenging my faith during many conversations at the kitchen table, outside the house, or just going about life. One day, he stopped mid-conversation, looked at my kitchen clock and turned to me,

"Auntie, look at the clock!" He said, a note of urgency in his voice. "It's ticking, but it will soon stop. And then what? The need is urgent, Auntie. What about those who still haven't accepted Christ when the clock stops?"

His words brought a fresh, solemn conviction and burden for me to faithfully make the gospel known.

The work in the Vila continued to grow, and our congregation also frequently went across the river to hold services and support the work there, principally in the slow process of constructing the physical building. We went step by step as and when resources came.

I focused on supporting and walking alongside the leadership in praying for the work, learning much from their faith, growth, and perseverance during fiery trials and battles to advance God's kingdom.

BETHEL MISSION FIELD

> *"Bethel (not the real name), near the Guamá River, became a municipality in 1943. According to IBGE (Brazilian census), its current population is approximately thirty thousand inhabitants.*
>
> *Bethel is an agricultural municipality with a mostly self-employed population. Young people seeking personal growth tend to migrate because of the fragile health, education and economic structures.*
>
> *In 2002, I, Zena Lima dos Santos and Santos, daughter of Pastor Raimundo Pastana dos Santos and Missionary Nazaré Lima dos Santos, set foot on the soil*

with my children to pioneer the work in the mission fields[29].

A member of the Baptist Church since the age of 15, I was eager to actively continue in the work of the Lord. With the absence of a Baptist Mission, a desire was planted in my heart to deploy a mission on Bethel soil. Desire turned into prayer and the search for support to start a Baptist work. While waiting for God's time to send the necessary support, I, Zena Santos, started out with small groups, worshipping God in my residence. In sowing the seed into this ground, we expected the Owner of the harvest to send us workers who would put their hand to the plough and not look back.

We were unaware of the great challenges ahead, but we fully understood that farming successfully requires much suffering and work and depends on sweat and skill. Even with poor soil or if the farmer is indisposed, he must continue toiling to avoid losing his harvest.

After going through several painful processes for the work started by a woman who wasn't sent by a convention instituted within the organizational parameters, the chosen who closed their eyes to the unfavourable circumstances and opened their hearts

---

[29] *Note: A pioneer is courageous enough to go where most are unwilling to and heed the call to places least inhabited.*

emerged, overflowing with love, and desiring to reach all peoples, including these.

The year 2013 was my first contact with Missionary Shirley from the nearby Baptist Congregation. The EBF (Holiday Bible School) was the first of many works carried out with Shirley's support. Subsequently, I reported on the history of my church-planting journey here during a meeting with Pastors, missionaries, and volunteers. Impacted by the written reports, Missionary Shirley went in search of financial support to build the temple, commencing a long journey that lasts until today. Shirley reflects sincere love, and describing her becomes easy whenever I come across the description of a servant in the sacred Scriptures. From planning to execution in building the Bethel Baptist Congregation, Shirley's conduct and testimony taught us how to tear down walls and build bridges. Beyond providing material resources, her ability to listen and intercede made her our Spiritual intercessor. Amid our great spiritual battles, Shirley ministered healing, deliverance, and restoration to us through God's Word and prayer. Many times, she carried us along when we lacked the strength to walk, and her presence during moments of great loss and affliction refreshed our souls.

Every achievement in the Bethel Mission Field contains the life, goods, and dedication of Missionary Shirley. Her love and attitude broke the barriers of distance, bringing many to the full knowledge of Christ. Together, we defied hell and entered a land dominated by evil to present Christ, the liberator. Her faith and deep, personal love for Jesus Christ inspire us to persevere with our Mission of loving the Lord and declaring that ONLY JESUS CHRIST SAVES!

OVERVIEW OF THE BAPTIST CONGREGATION IN BETHEL

The Baptist Congregation of Bethel started when Zena Lima dos Santos and Santos arrived in the municipality. She immediately noticed the lack of a church and the scarcity of social, educational, and spiritual works that could meet the needs of young people and children who were at the mercy of a degrading municipality steeped in vast poverty that left its residents vulnerable.

A series of works commenced aimed at inserting religious education into community activities to transform the various areas of human life in public spaces like schools. As the work gained visibility in society, it drew the attention of government officials, generating benefits, but also awakened opponents, resulting in persecution as previously available spaces were withdrawn and the urgent need for our own place arose. However, we lacked the resources because until then, we had no partnership or support.

Years of struggles later, as we were on the verge of giving up, Shirley appeared with knowledge and experience of similar challenges, moved by the Holy Spirit to give herself to make our long-standing dream come true. She drew other soldiers, donations, and voluntary offerings, making it possible to acquire an area and construct the temple within a neighbourhood deemed to be enemy territory.

Big battles were fought to implant the Kingdom of God, and my family suffered violence and immeasurable losses, but we are convinced that they in no way compare with the glory to be revealed in this place. Today, we have our own space. In a community of people without financial resources, dominated by drugs and criminality, much of what we have accomplished was only possible through the Lord's mighty hand on Shirley's life, generating in us an unshakable spirit. The harvest is great, and few are willing to go.

We glorify God the Father, for this life consecrated to the service of King Jesus." - Zena Santos, Evangelist.
Bethel Baptist Congregation

Made In Brazil

Today, the Bethel Baptist Congregation has a Sunday morning children's work and an evening service available to the community. There are few members, but a congregation of approximately 10 to 20 people regularly attends.

Missionary Aline has initiated a Saturday sports outreach that reaches out to children, teens, and young adults.

The congregation in the Vila regularly supports and organizes evangelistic events to impact the community. Several families have indicated a desire to know more, and we now have weekly Bible studies with six families and growing. We give God the glory and honour, knowing he will carry on to completion of the work he has begun.

Despite the intense battles, we hold onto his promise:

"I will build my church, and the gates of hell will not prevail against it." Matthew 16:18

By the end of 2019, we prepared to return to the UK for home assignment. We were waiting for Thalia's legal documents to come through when COVID-19 arrived on the scene, postponing our travel plans and turning all our lives around once again.

We were learning new lessons in God's school of life. We had just sold most of our belongings and moved into temporary accommodation in a very basic environment with limited internet. Then life went into Lockdown, and everything moved online, including school. We had to develop new routines, rhythms, and ways to do ministry.

Our residence throughout Lockdown was comparable to Elijah's experience of God's provision by the brook. We were isolated in a beautiful, safe place, surrounded by nature and a river, and as usual, God looked after every detail, providing several special memories of the Lockdown period. Life changed in many ways: I caught COVID and suffered from health problems in my lungs, fatigue, and other issues for months.

Our eventual return to the UK was far from straightforward. With more lockdowns, we were unable to see friends and family or secure long-term accommodation. It was a fresh roller coaster of trials, stress, and new lessons while God continued working out his plans and purposes, using the circumstances and events to locate us in an estate for which he had given me a burden when I was starting out in full-time ministry. God also confirmed that my time in Brazil was coming to an end, and despite praying and exploring going to another unreached people group elsewhere, that door didn't open. I was to do ministry in the UK for the time being.

I could share much about how God worked and led during this new season and what we will be involved in, but that's another story!

If you are clear about God's will for you, courageously press forward by faith. His presence will be with you, and that is really all you need.

Always live with these two certainties:

- Being aligned with God's will is essential
- He will be with you.

From there, everything else amounts to details along the great and wonderful adventure of life.

God's plans for the future are centred on the Cross. I am going to Heaven one day, and I intend to take as many people as possible with me.

CONCLUSION

This, my story and God's story is a small part of all he has done and what I have experienced. I write it hoping something would resonate, help, encourage and minister to you, wherever you are on life's journey.

God has been faithful and done beyond what I ever imagined, dreamt, or even thought possible. He gave me experiences and adventures and did amazing things that, as I shared, were often not easy but always worthwhile. I am deeply grateful for all he allowed me to go through; they have made me who I am today.

We often think we serve God to bless or help others, but the biggest lesson I learned is that God calls and allows us to serve him and experience situations so he can change us! Today's Shirley is not the Shirley who left the UK in 2003. I have been changed and now see life differently through the mission field's refining process. With my new perspective on life, I am convinced that my calling was not for what I could do for God but for what he wanted to do in me!

We don't have the final product yet, as the story is still being written. God continues to change and mould me in a step-by-step process. With each step, he reveals the next, and we move toward "becoming" and are transformed from glory into glory.

> *But we all, with unveiled face, beholding as in a mirror the glory of the Lord, are being transformed into the same image from glory to glory, just as by the Spirit of the Lord.* 2 Corinthians 3:18

We need the process as much as the product – the Lord wants our holiness, but he also wants to make us wholly his. My prayer continues to be:

> *"Lord, change me. Whatever you do, don't leave me the same. Make me like you. Make me forever yours."*

The impact of your ministry to people is directly proportionate to the time you spend with God. As the Psalmist shares in Psalm 27:4,

> *"One thing I have desired of the Lord,*
> *That will I seek:*
> *That I may dwell in the house of the Lord*
> *All the days of my life,*
> *To behold the beauty of the Lord,*
> *And to inquire in His temple."*

Conclusion

The place of intimacy at Christ's feet is where we get all our answers. Lord, keep me there in all the busyness of life!

God's will gets done when a person follows hard after his heart. He requires us to hold everything else loosely and seek hard after him. Without him, we can do NOTHING!

He desires that we know him intimately so that we become effective testimonies in our lives and witness.

> *"Within the veil, for only as thou gazest*
> *Upon the matchless beauty of his face*
> *Canst thou become a living revelation*
> *Of his great love, his untold grace[30]."*

Allow God to write your story, no matter how hard or difficult. I pray this testimony of how God has written mine challenges every reader to let God write yours by leading you along his amazing paths and plans for you. It will change you completely, but it's worthwhile.

Above all, I desire that you personally know God, the author and perfecter of our stories. May your hope be rescued and renewed as you receive his strength to keep going. Remember, he uses the weak things of this world and *will* use you. The secret is to yield like clay in the potter's hands and let him make you into his image, to the praise of his glory.

---

[30] *Within the Veil* – Hymn by FH Allen

I want the rest of my life to sing to him, to just be used as and when he wants, where and how he wants, and to be that instrument and arrow in his hand that hits its goal and leaves marks for eternity. Finally, I want to impact eternity and be a lasting legacy for the glory of God, and I pray you do the same!

I surrender all of my hopes and ambitions into his hands and give all that I am and have to him.

Will you give your ALL to Jesus today? Will you let him write your story and make you ALL he intended?

If you do not already know Jesus Christ as your Lord and Saviour, you don't have to wait any longer.

Here is a prayer to get you started on your journey:

Dear Lord,

> Thank you for dying on the Cross to free me from my sins. I am sorry for all the wrong things I have done. I turn to you now to receive your forgiveness and start walking in your ways.
>
> I give you my heart. Be my Lord and Saviour, fill me with the Holy Spirit and mould me into your image as I journey with you from now on.
>
> Thank you, Lord Jesus.
>
> Amen.

RECOMMENDED READING

The Street Children of Brazil: One Woman's Remarkable Story - by Sarah de Carvalho

---

[i] *Broken things, UCB August 9th, 1998*

[ii] https://www.biblestudytools.com/lexicons/greek/nas/parakletos.html

[iii] The Star Thrower. (2024, March 3). In *Wikipedia*. https://en.wikipedia.org/wiki/The_Star_Thrower

[iv] Christian Focus Publishing. All right reserved. Used with permission.

Printed in Great Britain
by Amazon